Formation in Spirit

Runic Trance & The Norse 'Holy Grail'

Appendixes

Table of Illustrations

Notes from the Publisher

Here we enter the domain of expertise of the Author. The volume and significance of what has been produced is downright short of being phenomenal. Rather than shorten it or publish only those parts which are deemed accessible to everyone and trimming out the advanced theories, concepts and content we have opted to include them all with only making structural changes.

What the author has given us is breath-taking, with information and knowledge based in actual wisdom on so many topics of the mind, consciousness, awareness, perception and senses that we were left short of words. In here, everyone will find invaluable insights ranging from what the Spirit actually is, how it was formed and why it has been formed down to manipulation and enhancement of consciousness, mastering perception, enhancing the sense, trance states, how the realms of mind function, why they function in that manner and many more.

Unfortunately, due to the vast nature of the submitted manuscript we have had to divide the original book into several volumes. It was either that or editing out the more advanced materials. We felt that doing so would rob this work of its intrinsic uniqueness and value and have hence opted to split it across several volumes. We hope that this decision proves to be welcomed by Rúnaldrar's readers. It is with great pleasure that we present you with one of the most impressive written works on this subject to date.

Notes from the Author

In these books, we are going to be looking at what we in the modern age call the 'spirit', that which our ancestors called the Óðr (or Óðr, or Óð), the mind, how our perceptions work, the influence of memory, the ancestral and briefly upon the impact of emotion. We will look at consciousness, awareness and the senses, how to shape them, expand them and develop them to new heights and boost perception beyond the coarse physical reality. You will learn mental discipline and exercises once taught to the young who exhibited talent for the runes in the old families as they unlocked the potentials stirring dormant within the Indo-European blood lines.

Unlike '*The Breath of Oðin Awakens*', the teachings from the Sagas, Eddas and Traditional records are much less prominent. They are used only briefly to reference the key concepts which are in turn contextualised from traditional teachings, guidance of the Vanir and Æsir and placed in modern context by means of psychology and scientific understandings. Hence the reliance on Eddic sources and text is somewhat less present in this and the following titles. We also have more material from the Seidr side of the craft as well as traditional teachings than in the former. I hope that this will enable both traditionalists and modern students alike to pick up the materials within and make practical use of them.

Having said all the above, we will be sticking to the pure Norse concepts, definitions of the Self and goal of preparation for the mastery of the Norse Self in our pursuit of learning to unleash proper Galdr.

That is, after all, the ultimate goal: mastering and practically applying High Galdr.

Thus we now enter the domain of the Gift of Húnir: the Spirit (Óðr). Let me hence take you through a wonderful journey of discovery of the inner potential of our consciousness, reasoning (Hugr), memories (Minni) and perception where neither space nor time are impairments to our reach. Fasten your mental and spiritual seatbelts; this is going to be quite a trip!

Note that this title introduces some extremely complex abstract concepts. It is important to read through them and reflect on them but not to worry if you struggle understanding them intellectually. If some seem illogical it is simply due to the intellect and experiential knowledge lacking. In order to remedy that, simply focus on practicing and doing the practical exercises. As your skill grows so will your awareness and consciousness. Then return to and re-read the theoretical parts as they will then make more sense and shed new light on what you are doing in your practical work, even as far as helping you iron out any issues you might have. This is unfortunately the only way to learn and grow. Think of it as a cycle in which your first perusal of the theoretical will shed light on the practical exercises which will in turn widen your perceptive insights. This will in turn shed even more light on the theoretical. The loop is repeated until full mastery is gained. It is a gradual process but if you do it persistently, you will see yourself grow in power, skill, ability and know-ledge each and every step of the way.

The process may seem rather laborious but other than having someone expand your consciousness directly, there is no other way to achieve this mastery. On the bright side, however, it is achievable by anyone willing to put in the time and effort. And be sure to always return to the foundational work even when you think you have outgrown it. Each time you do, it will be read/seen in a new light which will provide additional insights.

Definitions of Norse Terms

Önd – Part of the psycho-spiritual construct of the Self as viewed in Norse mysticism and mythology, the Önd sits at the apex of the spiritual level of the Self and can be loosely described as 'The Breath of Oðin Awakens'[1].

Óðr (or Óðr, or Óð) – Part of the psycho-spiritual Self sitting at the apex of the mental part of the Self, it can be loosely thought of as the conscious awareness or totality of the spirit.

Hugr – The Hugr is often thought of as the reasoning or logic part of the mind, sometimes as the mind itself and often as the intellect or intellectual capacity of the mind. Essentially it is the manifestation of the active characteristics of the Spirit (Óðr).

Minni – The polar opposite of the Hugr and often thought of as the root of memory, the Minni is actually the individual record of one's experiences and acts as an anchor point for those events.

Hamr – The Hamr is the energy body, often described as the blueprint of the physical.

Lik – Part of the psycho-spiritual Self sitting at the apex of the energetic part of the Self, the Lik is the complete physical body as a result of the fusion of matter and spirit via the medium of energy. When talking about the Lik we include everything which is part of it, including the energetic and spiritual elements as well as the typically physical ones such as blood, DNA, nervous system and so forth.

Sal – Part of the psycho-spiritual self sitting at the bottom of the energetic part of the Self, the Sal is often loosely translated as the 'shadow'. In effect, it is the complimentary opposite of the Hamr.

Heimdall – One of the principle Gods in Norse mythology, Heimdall was described as the white god or whitest of the gods. He is linked to light and the pure power thereof. He possesses the resounding horn Gjallarhorn, which he will sound at the time of Ragnarök. He is the god responsible for originating the social classes of mankind and imbuing these three classes of humans with increasing degrees of divinity.

The Æsir – This refers to the clan of Gods from Asgard, typically associated with the divine aspects of spiritual origin. They are wielders of the Galdr sciences (use of runes and their correct applications) and have strong connections with the spiritual, awareness, intellect, mind, knowledge and the sciences.

The Vanir – The Vanir refers to the clan of Gods from Vanaheim, typically associated with the natural order of things and having strong connections with nature, the world and the physical as it moves towards the spiritual. They are wielders of Seidr crafts (sorcery, divination, soothsaying, shamanistic practices, herbal medicines and so forth).

Yggdrasil – The mythical Ash tree that is home to the nine worlds in Norse cosmology. It is also thought of as being the foundation of the cosmos itself and everything within it.

Egil's Saga – Otherwise termed in Iceland as the Egla, this is an Icelandic Saga dating back to 1240 AD, which details the life of Egil Skallagrimsson a farmer, Viking and poet.

Muspelheim – Muspelheim was the first world to be formed out of the great emptiness called Ginnungagap. It is a realm of flame, fires, light and explosive power unreachable by any not native to it.

Húnir (Hœnir) – One of the Æsir Gods, he helped create mankind along with Oðin and Lóðurr. He gave the first man and woman Óðr and hence imbued them with Spirit. He is also one of the Gods who survives Ragnarök and gains prophetic powers thereafter.

Njörðr – Vanir God of the Sea, he is the father of Freya and Frey and was one of the hostages exchanged in the Æsir-Vanir war. It is said he will return to head the Vanir after Ragnarök.

Lóðurr (Lóð or Lóðr) – Lóðurr is a mysterious God, whom academics seem unable to accept other than trying (and failing) to identify him with Loki or even Freyr. He gives the first man and woman blood and hence health, in other words flesh or physicality.

Ragnarök – Also known as the Twilight of the Gods, this final battle was foretold in the Völuspá (stanza 41). It describes the ultimate fate of the Gods themselves.

Ætts – Meaning 'clan', it can also refer to related grouping of concepts, individuals or sets of people. It is sometimes referred to as kin-Ætts which would be used in terms of a grouping of related people. For instance, Ætts in terms of individuals would include related individually such as family, whereas kin-Ætts would expand this to a wider set of relations such as an entire clan.

Norns – This typically refers to the Jotun (giantess) sisters Urð, Verðandi and Skuld who weave the threads of fate for men and gods alike. They also draw water from the Well of Urð and collect sands from around it to pour on the Yggdrasil to prevent it from rotting. The word Norn can also refer to the concept of the fate weaver attached to individuals at birth which could be either good or bad, weaving either a fortunate or unfortunate fate for that individual.

Niflheim – One of the Nine Worlds in Norse Cosmology, Niflheim is a world of primordial ice and cold, sometimes also called the mist world.

Fylgja – Part of the archetypal level of the Self, the Fylgja is a spirit which binds to the individual, becoming a part of him/her upon birth. It is always inherited down the ancestral lines and carries experiential essence and memories and powers of the former Self's embodiment. The Fylgja forms into either animal, humanoid or geometric form depending on evolutionary progress of both the individual and itself.

Kin-Fylgja – Similar to the Fylgja, this overarching spirit carries the experiential essences of the entire family line, the sum resulting from the entire ancestral lines up to the current point. It attaches to the eldest male of the family line and communicates primarily through the females of the line.

Hamingja – The Hamingja is part of the archetypal level of the Self. It manifests as an energetic organ in the individual which stores the Megin (power) it produces from various runic and life energies (see 'The Breath of Oðin Awakens')[2].

Wyrd and Ørlǫg – This refers to fate or rather threads of fate as they flow through creation. Cosmically, Ørlǫg is seen as infinite fibres of energetic substance flowing throughout all existence. From a human perspective, these fibres appear to flow through Creation but also through individuals, gods and all life forms, setting the path they will follow over the course of their existence. However, when viewed from a Cosmic perspective, all things in Creation flow through the fibres. The Wyrd refers to these threads on a larger scale such as for humanity as a whole, individual races and clans while Ørlǫg refers to how these threads manifest on the individual level. The Wyrd is formed by the Norns and the Ørlǫg is build from the Wyrd based on individual's power, fate and evolutionary needs by the Fylgja.

Óðrerir (Odhrærir, Óðrørir) – This refers to the container or cauldron which holds the sacred mead. Its equivalent is the legend of the 'Holy Grail' in Arthurian mythology and the 'Holy Chalice' in Christian mythology. The Óðrerir may well have been the inspiration for these later myths.

THE NORSE TRADITION – HERITAGE OF THE INDO-EUROPEANS

It is impossibly difficult to determine the full extent of or to search out all sources of the Norse tradition. Most pre-date the widespread availability of writing, while others were passed exclusively from one generation to the next orally. The main sources of know-ledge left to us in this modern day and age are found in the Eddas and the Sagas.

THE EDDAS

The term 'Eddas' comes from Old Norse and it is used by modern-day students and academics to refer to two main Icelandic literary works that serve as the basis of our knowledge of Norse mythology, tradition, teachings and history.

There are two primary Eddas, both written during the 13th Century in Iceland. The first set is grouped under the label 'Poetic Eddas', which predate even the Viking Age, and come from an unknown source. They are divided into two sections; the first is a narration of the creation, destruction and rebirth of the world and provides the mythology of the Norse deities as well. The second is a set of legends relating to Norse heroes, kings and wise men.

The Poetic Eddas were incorporated into the Codex Regius written during the 13th century. Unfortunately, it was not until the mid-1600s that the Codex resurfaced in the hands of Brynjólfur Sveinsson, a bishop to the Church of Iceland in Skálholt. Brynjólfur was also a scholar at heart, hence his fascination with the old myths and legends! It is he who collected and produced this compilation of Old Norse mythology and heroic poems into the Eddas. However, it is widely accepted that he was not their author and so they were not labelled after him. He gifted his findings to King Christian IV of Denmark in manuscript form, thus earning it the name Codex Regus, which was then preserved in the Royal Library until 1971 when a formal return was made to Iceland.

The second Eddas were compiled from traditional oral sources and (theorised to be derived from) an unknown set of Eddas often referred to as the Elder Eddas by Icelandic scholar Snorri Sturluson (dated from the 14th century). He collated these literary works under the label of Prose Eddas. Like the Poetic Eddas, the Prose Eddas also describe in detail the creation, destruction and rebirth of the world, Norse mythology and life. Due to his background and the time period in which Snorri lived, the 'Christianisation' of certain concepts and legends are to be found in this text. Nonetheless, it does provide an invaluable and rich account of the Norse tradition and, just as importantly, how it was recounted over the generations.

Scholars have long held the view that the Poetic Eddas, and therefore the Prose Eddas, came from a much older source. The rediscovery of what is known as the Elder Eddas helped confirm that suspicion. The Elder Eddas are comprised of the Pagan poems and teachings that were later hinted at in Snorri's Prose Eddas.

Many translations from Old Norse can be found and the number thereof seems to increase steadily over time. One key point to keep in mind is that the Eddas are complex literary works detailing the Norse tradition through poetry and prose. Accordingly, when reading various translations, different terms and words are often found to express the same underlying concept or similar words are used to describe totally different ones. Add to this the fact that many Old Norse terms have no equivalents in modern day languages, and it becomes vitally important to read in between the lines, so to speak, referring back to the concept rather than relying strictly on the words themselves. A literal, legalistic reading that has become completely engrained in the modern readers' minds will fail to capture the actual meanings, concepts and knowledge held within the Eddas.

Aside from those mentioned, other so-called Eddas can be found. These are typically adaptations in use by specific groups based on either the Prose or Poetic Eddas. The key point to note, however, is that those are adaptations.

The translations of the Prose and Poetic Eddas that have been used as source materials for this work can be found in both the references and further reading sections. Modern day adaptations and/or derivatives are not used.

THE SAGA(S)

Unlike the Eddas, the term Saga (story) refers to one of the many stories, poems, legends and so forth. Not all the Sagas made it into the Eddas. Individual Sagas might have not been discovered until a much later, post-Eddas compilation period.

These Sagas are individual tales in prose or poetic form detailing historical events of heroic deeds, tales or important persons (a great many of them Vikings, Pagans or even sometimes Christians), bishops, saints and even legendary heroes. Many of the Sagas include tales of kings, special individuals (such as the Egil Sagas used in this text), and even territorial historic events ranging from the Nordic countries to the British Isles, France and even North America (Canada in particular)[3]. Their main characteristic is that they are a historical statement or tale (that is the literal meaning of the term Saga). This has raised much speculation as the intellectual machinery attempts to digest material that is these days considered to be supernatural or metaphysical.

This range of subject matter is simply due to the fact that these records were, more often than not, kept within individual families, transmitted orally or simply brought from a different territory. Remember, the Old Norse people (Indo-Europeans) existed long before the Viking age and had to survive forced Christianisation, dispersion of territories, hostile natural environments, and so forth. In other words, these Sagas provided additional insights into the traditions, mythology, legends and teachings that were initially transmitted orally and then, once writing became widely available, were from time to time published. Even to this date, however, many of the Sagas have never been published and are kept from public view for a variety of reasons. Some of these reasons are of a very practical nature. In Iceland, for instance, these stories are considered to be part of the national heritage, hence books or manuscripts that are valued as family heirlooms, if known about, would be confiscated by the state on the basis of it being a national treasure. This is somewhat of an over-simplification but is an example of one of the many reasons why a lot of these Sagas never have (and most probably never will) see the light of public accessibility or dissemination. Others might hold deep-seated hereditary knowledge, which, more often than not, requires specific genetic and energetically transmitted capabilities to be of any use. This is the case with the higher mysteries bestowed upon the Jarls by Heimdall.

Fortunately, many sagas are available for public consumption, and they do provide an exceptional insight into the wisdom and traditions of our ancestors. In this work, the Sagas are used to illustrate and gain further insights into teachings from older sources, be they part of the oral tradition or those in the Eddas[4].

This seeming endless diversity of sources is what makes studying the Old Norse tradition wildly exciting and fascinating beyond expectation, yet also insanely frustrating. Each Saga and Edda can expand our understanding, yet finding the relevant ones can be a most noteworthy challenge, in addition to actually understanding the knowledge therein once it is found! Nevertheless, gaining a solid foundation into the tradition is key; it is after all part of our heritage and is what empowers us. The appendices will provide more references and recommended reading. Fear not, however — all Eddas and Sagas relevant to the topics and teachings in this book have been included; for without basing such teachings in the actual texts and other sources of heritage they would hold no validity per se. It is of vital importance to work with these Eddas and Sagas as the foundation upon which we build our spiritual heritage.

INTRODUCING... HIGH GALDR

The Spirit of Húnir is the second of the four keys required for mastery of High Galdr. The knowledge and teachings provided in both Parts 1 and 2 of the Spirit of Húnir Awakens provide the key skills and perceptual abilities required for both the manipulation of runic energies (and currents) and the mental or spiritual parts of the Self. Awareness and understanding of Spirit itself, enhancing of the senses, mastery of perception, trances, the first steps in being multi-dimensional, practical understanding and mastery of intent are all but a few of the essential steps in mastering the Self at this abstract level of existence and making use of it in our daily lives.

The mastery of the Self, as defined by our Norse ancestry, unlocks the potential for Galdr. This involves the awakening of the Megin-filled breath (Önd), which has already been covered in the previous publication, then developing the flow of conscious awareness through the Spirit (Óðr) which is the focus of this work.

WHAT IS GALDR?

The practice of Galdr is fundamental to the Æsir and was 'taught' to humankind when Heimdall revealed the runes to humanity. Subsequently, other teachers from the realms of Asgard came forth to various gifted individuals to teach them more advanced applications of runic practices. Long ago, Galdr was taught to the Vanir by Oðin himself, just as they revealed the arts of Seidr to him. Interestingly, this exchange is an excellent illustration of the practical applications of X Gjöf (Gebo) (the principle of a gift requiring a gift) even at that divine level!

So what is Galdr? One can define it as the uttering of runes, runic formulae, runic chants, the vocalisation of runes and bind-runes accompanied by their tracing or carving.

In Midgard, and specifically in relation to humans, these arts were used in a severely limited fashion, which essentially reduced Galdr to vocal-isation of the runes. It became a meagre chanting, visualising and tracing of the runes (for the sake of brevity, formulae, chants and bind-runes are herein included when mentioning 'runes'). Worse yet, the concept of Galdr itself has been fused with that of Seidr. This merging was not done through a harmonious blending of the two arts, but rather aspects of the one were muddled into the other. The underlying fundamentals of Galdr gradually shifted from pure mysticism to one of ritualistic application. In the process, it lost the true power of Galdr itself, which wound up as a shadow of its former potential.

Some might argue that elements of Seidr are needed in Galdr, such as the induction of trance states found within Seidr as being essential to the effective use of Galdr. This is both partly correct and incorrect. While it is true that trance mastery is essential to Galdr, it is incorrect to assume that Seidr is required. Galdr itself is used to induce a trance state, which can at times even surpass those achieved via Seidr (in terms of practicality, not potential). This stems from the mystical aspects of Galdr and is the reason why it was deemed in days long past to be the sacred science of the Gods.

The 'High Galdr' series seeks to bring back the knowledge and the tools to practice the sacred aspects of Galdr. Due to its nature, many will flock to it. Some will seek to master it and others will seek to abuse it. To the former, all that remains to be said is be persistent and practice; even partial success and minor achievements expand the Self, providing phenomenal gains. Once fully mastered, there will be nothing left that anyone in Midgard can teach. For the latter, a warning: even though High Galdr can be misused, it is vital to remain aware that the Gods protect their mysteries and they them-selves throw hurdles in the path and practices of those who are seeking to harm their people, their creation and the cosmic order of things for which they are responsible. Not much else needs to be said on that subject other than to confirm that no matter how hard those who would abuse them try, these sacred mysteries will always evade mastery.

In these pages, you will find instructions to take the next step. It will assist in uncovering the mysteries of this science and awaken the parts of the Self, moving them towards the divine, and eventually lead you to uttering the Galdr across multiple levels of reality (both subjectively and objectively). This will free the mind of all the baggage that inhibits our heritage from blooming, enabling you to learn the rune and each rune's specific energy patterns, condense them into reality, and finally unleash them. The microcosmic Yggdrasil within our bodies and the macrocosmic Yggdrasil will be brought into a synchronous harmony as the Self unfolds into its divine birth right.

Now is the time to become aware of the Óðr;
Now, the 'Spirit of Húnir' awakens.
May the Óðr shine bright from within!

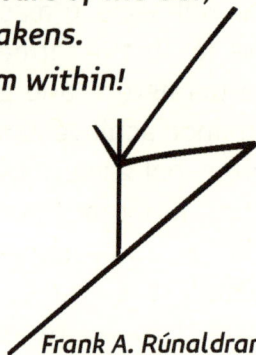

Frank A. Rúnaldrar

THE SPIRIT OF HÚNIR (HŒNIR)

It is with great pleasure that we are bringing you the second title in the High Galdr series. In the Spirit of Húnir Awakens, the focus is on the mental level of the Self, namely the spirit (Óðr), Hugr and Minni which in modern day terminology can loosely be termed the Spirit, Logic/Reason/Mind and Memory.

Topics covered in this title are extensive — exceedingly so. The focal point is the mastery of the mind and spirit and setting yourself free of socially imposed limitations and conditioning. Some very important skill sets are developed across the two volumes which comprise this title. Working through them, you will develop an actual understanding of what spirit is, how it was formed and why, as well as start to develop an insight into how the Holy Norse Trinity created Ask and Embla (the first man and woman). Here, we are introduced into this highly abstract mystery as we see how Húnir took the Önd gifted by Oðin and, out of its activity, bestowed the spirit (Óðr) on our ancestors. The practical work allows us to take the spirit (Óðr) and start mastering both it and all the essential abilities it provides us with which are required for use in actual Galdr.

You will learn about increasing your sensory percept-ions, widening awareness, setting the Hugr raven to flight, grounding perceptions in other realities picked up by your growing awareness, shapeshifting the spirit (Óðr) into the runes, the impact of language on your mind, how your perceptions of your social self limit your mind, the reality behind the myth of the so-called subconscious, evidence in the sciences and what impact technology has on your abilities. In the second book of this title, the practical work delves even further. You will be learning about pure thought and how to free your mind of linguistic limitations, how to free yourself of the 'mind thief', reclaim your energies, the secrets to visualisation (and how to make them work!), how the mental level of reality and thought work, their relations to energetic realities and how they are used to manifest, how to augment your thinking capacity and give your thoughts that extra punch they need for Galdr and manifestation, runic trance dancing and, most importantly of all, you will learn about intent. Specifically, you will learn what it is and how to actually unleash and empower your intent, thereby tapping into this most mysterious force which gave rise to all things in reality, ultimately leading to Óðrerir: The Norse 'Holy Grail'.

THE MENTAL LEVEL OF REALITY

Understanding the Mental & Spiritual Level of Reality

In order to influence our own or other peoples' spirit (Óðr) or the level of reality in which it functions (the mental level of creation), we need to understand the rules which operate at that level. While some may call them laws, the term 'principals' is a much better fit.

All thoughts at that level of creation are abstractions of what we understand as thoughts within the human mind-set. Words, typically in one's native language, are the default tools for human thinking. There are a rare few, however, who are set to a different default. Some of them think in images, similar to daydreaming. Other individuals think in sounds or sensations and some in even rarer cases think in terms of flavours, smells or numbers. All these manifestations of thoughts are just that: manifestations. As soon as one gives shape to a thought, it starts to gather energy and fits into that shape. The moment that happens, you have moved from the mental level of reality into the next which is that of energy and matter.

It is extremely rare for an individual to naturally think in terms of pure thought but with training, this can be achieved. What is meant by 'pure thought' is thought without shape, word, symbol, form or sensory information of any sort whatsoever. In this type of thinking, you get pure thought as a concept flowing forth, a meaning without context or definition and an abstraction without shape. The only way in which we can conceptualise this type of pure thought is as an essence of the thought itself which can be sensed (but not felt!) as flowing within the thought itself. This may not make much sense when attempting to express it in words but in practice, when perception of pure thought is accessed, it makes perfect sense. Such pure thoughts can carry intent and meaning across realities and levels of reality. You can pack so much significance into a single thought that it can hold boundless knowledge. Accessing and using such pure thought is what we are aiming to achieve with our practices, for pure thought is the only way in which one can unlock the knowledge of the rune one is working with and the knowledge held within our DNA.

UNDERSTANDING THOUGHT

So what is a thought? The best way to describe it is as a piece of information, a meaning, a concept. At its purest level, it is essentially a unit of knowledge. All living things with awareness generate and create thought, as do all things with Spirit (Óðr). Things without awareness do not, nor do dead things. Once dead, perceptive awareness fades until it is no more. As it does, thought and the process of thinking fades with it.

Whilst alive, the living organism will generate, receive and process thought in one or more ways. For humans, the undisciplined mind is like a radio that constantly broadcasts on multiple levels. What is being broadcast depends on the person but typically it can well be described as a cacophony of diverse thoughts based on that person's current focus of awareness. The range, complexity and diversity of thought is entirely dependant on the level of intellect of the broadcaster-receiver.

How thought functions on the mental level of reality

It is important to keep in mind that the mental level of reality has no space. There is no concept of it, nor any manifestation of it. Hence everything is one thing and all things are in one place. It is highly dynamic, constantly redefining itself and all things within it. As soon as there is any form of perception or new input, everything will shift and be redefined in some way or other. Only the things that we focus on will 'exist' at any point in time. Time exists there, although it is a different type of time than we understand here in Midgard. At the quantum level, time is 'Never', 'NOW' or 'Eternity'. There are a multitude of

NOWs and Eternities but there is only one Never. All these can be described as prime states of time in our language rather than time itself.

Each thought starts off either being generated or being received. As soon as thought is generated, it is pulsed outwards on the mental level of reality. Anyone or anything in harmony with that thought will receive it and process it, thereby attaching new meaning and new life to it. Then it pulses out yet again. As you can imagine, the mental level can get very busy indeed. But one important factor needs to be known about it, and this comes from a practical knowledge rather than an intellectualised type. The mental reality works differently than the reality that we understand — it is more like the quantum field. When you look at the mental level, you are 'alone' in it. You will only see yourself and those things you have actual connections with, along with those thoughts you think and whatever echoes with them. Unless you are thinking of so and so, you will not perceive or mentally interact with them. Hence "out of thought out of mind" is an excellent saying to remember when working at this level of reality.

In effect, the rule is not that 'we are all one' as modern-day mankind is obsessed with but rather that 'I am everything and everything which is at one with me is me'. Anything which is not a part of you simply does not exist for you and since it does not exist for you, it just does not exist. You need to bring it into your mental 'space' if you want it to exist. This is why it is important to interact at both the energetic and Midgard levels, as here that rule does not apply. It is a different level of reality with rules of its own where people and things that we cannot even conceive of, let alone think off, CAN interact with us, sometimes even if we do not want them to.

'LIKE ATTRACTS LIKE' PRINCIPLE & MANIFESTATION OF THOUGHT

Everyone has heard of this one, or should have! It is a principle of the mental level of reality which is, more often than not, mis-assigned to other levels. On the mental side of things, it is absolute. When you think of something, you not only attract it but also attract all those other thoughts, concepts and ideas which are like it. This is a fundamental principle for how this entire level of reality works. There is no such thing as 'opposites attract' on the mental. Instead like will attract like, or 'each calls out to his or her own', if you prefer. This is the origin of 'trains of thoughts' where one thinks of one idea and a connected thing will pop into one's mind, then a third and so forth.

This principle of the mental level of reality is VITAL to grasp for it allows the imagination to act as a key to actuality. When we start working with a rune, providing we have certain bits of information about it, we 'think' it. Thinking a rune means that we sense it by imagining it and then imbue it with all the meaning and information that we have about it. Do that often and it will attract things that are like it, namely the actual runic energy and rune stream. Those who are taught these fundamentals are thus provided with an important key to shaping reality. For those who fail to grasp it, however, that very same key can turn into a nightmare. How so? Take a moment and think about the most annoying, negative person you know — someone who moans about everything time after time after time, such as not having enough money. What are they sending out in their thinking? According to the 'like attracts like' principle, they are broadcasting 'I lack enough money' at the mental level of reality . Because they do it constantly, their thoughts gather more and more momentum, building energy and intensity. Then BAM! A lack of money will manifest in their lives. As far as the energetic realities are concerned, they got exactly what they sought. This is further compounded because now that there is a manifested lack of money, they begin to obsess over not having money again. This in turn echoes as 'lack of money' across the mental level of reality and the vicious cycle repeats again.

Fixing this type of problem is not about clearing out negative energy — you cannot clear out a natural manifestation. It can only be fixed through clearing out that person's mental level of reality AND changing their thinking patterns. The loop needs to be broken in order to stop manifesting that which is unwanted. Unfortunately, such loops are notoriously difficult to break and even harder to keep away from. More on doing so will be covered at a later time.

Everyone is subject to these mental and energetic principles if they live in Midgard regardless of whether they know about them or like them. Creation is ruthless.

For the time being, the important thing to focus on is how we use these principles in our rune work!

It is essentially simple: you think of something, feel and sense it. Then enliven it over and over again and it will attract the actual thing you are thinking off, eventually manifesting it. The better skilled at this you become, the quicker the manifestation and the less obstruction to manifestation there is. If something is not working, change the way you are thinking about it. We will use these techniques extensively in our rune work, which in turn will broaden the mind and make it even easier to apply them effectively. For future reference, this is known as the 'Principle of Thinking'.

Interrelation of energy and thought – first stages of manifestation

Each thought contains the energy of the generator and the thing it represents. For example, if you think of an apple, it will contain the energy you gave it when thinking of it in addition to energy which causes it to be shaped as an apple. This will also contain the pure thought concept of what an apple is as well as whatever meaning you assign to it. Consider, too, that an apple for you will not be the same thing as an apple for someone else because we each experience it in slightly different ways, ranging from what it looks like, what it tastes like, our liking or disliking of the apple and all our memories of apples! It is the generation and association of meanings with perceptual information (including memory of ancestral perceptions of it) which is vital to the nature of the thought. This

7

is why so-called 'artificial intelligence' (AI) will never be able to replicate or generate thought, coupled with the fact that it has no Spirit (Óðr). It may be able to tap into the perceptions of others through limited sharing of information but it is not capable of perceiving and attaching actual meaning as an Spirit (Óðr) would.

This also serves well to remind us just how individualistic a thought actually is when generated and becomes even more so when perceived. There is an infinite number of perceptual variations.

All this, of course, has been viewed without looking at the impact of time. Let's return to our apple example for a moment. An apple as you see and experience it right now will be very different from how you might perceive the same apple a few moments later. We seldom notice minute time differences because the human condition does not include such perceptions. However, we readily notice the effects time has on things over longer periods. How will that same apple taste a few days later? A week later? A month? As you keep in mind the context of time, your perceptive mechanism will expand to the point where smaller and smaller time effects become more noticeable.

Thus far, we have examined the effects of looping thought patterns. Once those patterns have been recognized, one can see how obsessive-compulsive behaviours, ingrained habits, fears, obsessions and so forth emerge. They are all the result of thoughts which have been looped so many times that they acquire an energetic mass in their own right — a type of mental gravity if you like. Once they have gained this dimensionality, they will propagate the loop in order to keep the energy incoming for as long as possible. Such thoughts are often referred to as 'thought forms'. When you have a situation where thought and energy are intermixed, you have shifted away from the mental level of reality and moved into the scope of the energetic level. There are countless degrees of existence in-between these two and how close something is to one side or the other will depend entirely on its mental gravity.

Once mental gravity gains momentum, something fascinating takes place–the thought loses some of its native dimensionality. It is now subjected to the rules of space, shape and form and hence is subject to interpretation. It will have added to it an infinitude of possible interpretations in addition to its infinitude of perceptions. At this point it is gaining dimension-ality but, as a result, it is also becoming more restricted. In other words, it has gained an energetic dimension which now is combined with the original thought (or thought patterns). The mental gravity is merged with an emerging coalescing energy. Because of the energetic dimensionality AND expanding meaning, it will now gravitate to those in tune with both or either of these dimensions (mental or energetic). However, if you are in tune with the conceptual or pure thought behind a thought form (the mental dimensionality), you will attract it by virtue of the principal of thoughts. BUT if you are not tune with its energetic part (the mental gravity), this might last only for a brief period of time because it is only a partial harmonisation. In other words, you can have a type of sympathy to the thought element of it but not the energetic yet. In those cases, its pull towards you and yours to it will be partial. However, if you have sympathy to the thought parts of it AND the energetic frequency or type, you will experience a full complete pull (or attraction) to this thought form.

Time comes into play due to the energetic gravity. We will cover this at a later point in time in much more detail but for now, keep in mind that just as thoughts gain gravity by way of energisation, energy itself gains gravity by condensation. In other words, the more energy you pack and the more solidly you do so, the greater the energetic gravity. This type of gravity is what modern day science is obsessed with. When looking at what it terms 'standard' concepts of gravity and the new quantum gravity, however, it struggles with the concept that gravity changes in nature but not manifestation. For our purposes, we can look at this phenomenon of gravity from its very source throughout all of its manifestations.

Mind Scattering
Internal Dialog

Thanks to our constant exposure to information overload, life stressors, excessive responsibilities, a narrowing of mental scope, overexposure to emotional stimulus, and many other environmentally-imposed destructive habits, our thoughts are pushed and pulled in all directions, constantly stimulating our brains. It is no wonder we cannot achieve expansion of conscious awareness — we are constantly being diverted left, right and centre, wasting all our energy and resources. This is why stilling the mind and putting a stop to (or at least pausing) our internal dialogue is an essential skill to develop. Even a few minutes will help provide a vast amount of energy and mental resources for better use. Gradually, as we keep persevering at silencing this internal dialogue, those resources begin to build up until we reach a trigger point and our minds become able to see, sense and interact with energy and other things directly. Until then, we must persevere in our practices no matter how hard or how frustrating it all becomes.

ESSENTIALS OF THOUGHT CONTROL

It is now time to practice getting a grip on all those millions of billions of thoughts passing through our minds, siphoning out our spirit (Óðr) energy. Start by sitting down and taking a deep breath. Relax your body and allow the world around you to fade into insignificance. Allow thoughts to rise in your mind, simply observe them. If you notice yourself trying to interact or engage with them, stop and allow them to flow on their own. You are not engaging with them, trying to direct them, or even trying to stop them from occurring. Just observe.

Quick Steps

1. Sit down and take a deep breath. Relax allow the world around you to fade.
2. Let your thoughts rise in your mind but rather than interact with them (or get involved with them), just observe them. This might be a little tricky at first because we are so used to flowing with our thoughts but just relax and allow them to pass in and out of your mind without engaging with them.
3. Observe how they pass. Feel yourself separate from them, acting as the passive observer

rather than the active thinker.

4. As soon as you notice yourself getting pulled back into thinking them, interrupt it and silently stay STOP.

5. As you observe, you will see that the flow of thought slows down, that it takes just a little tiny bit longer between one thought and the next. The more proficient you get, the longer this gap will become. Do not think about these gaps but just observe them passively.

Upon practicing this, you will notice a sharpening of the mind. A type of detachment will occur where you are no longer totally engaged with the thoughts attempting to flow through your mind. Thoughts will come less often when unwanted but will flow faster and less interruptible than before when you want them to do so. You will find that when you focus your consciousness on something, it will be easier to maintain that focus, penetrating deeply into what you are focussing on with ease. Whereas you previously had thousands of meaningless thoughts bubbling forth in a cloud, each one siphoning out a little energy at a time, now there is a huge freeing of mind's energy resources.

As you disentangle from 'random' thoughts attempting to gain a foothold in your mind, you will notice that the energy spared from engaging with them can be redirected with focus into selected single thoughts that you actually want to work with. This causes all the energy which would have otherwise been siphoned off to instead be poured into your thought which has purpose. This empowered thought then has sufficient energy and dynamics to cut through the masses upon masses of weak mental clouds on the mental level of reality as would a sharp sword, or a laser beam striking at a specific desired target.

DEEPER STATES OF MIND

By stilling the mental chit-chat in our minds, we can easily enter deeper mental states typically called trances. All that is required is for us to still our thoughts and focus on whatever we desire to be the subject matter of the trance. This is a little different from widely understood trance states which involve just going quiet. Here, we are focussing this deepened state of mind on something, somewhere or some concept. In our case, we will naturally focus it on the runes, our Self, parts of our Self and various abstract concepts covered in the Norse Mysteries.

It is important to understand how information flows during these deeper states of mind. Here we are restricting, if not eliminating, thought. Some of you might wonder how do you develop knowledge, communicate and understand or even process ideas without the use of thought. It is a common misnomer that thought is the source of any of these things. As we will see later on when looking at intent, we have what is called 'pure thought' to do these things. The use of pure thought and intent without having to think was the original way for mankind to do all these things. It was only when language became such a dominant factor in our lives that this was forgotten and a switch to thinking in words took place. When dealing with pure thought, there is no thought per se. It is really an abstraction that we are dealing with. Due to this abstraction, many additional possibilities open up, for instance millions and millions of pages of knowledge can be transmitted into a single instance of such an abstraction to the point where both the mind-reason (Hugr) and spirit (Óðr) can be overwhelmed by it. Typically, we have one thought carrying one piece of information but with pure thought, that limit is completely removed. Another possibility which opens up is the communication across species. Thought or rather how you form it or its pattern is unique to each species and to a lesser extent to the races within the species. This means communicating across species is practically impossible with normal thinking. You simply cannot think as a bird, cat or dog would. When working with pure thought, there is no 'thinking per se' and these limitations fade. The final advantage worth mentioning is when dealing with concepts which are not defined in language. When thinking, you would have to think around this limitation, trying to fit or coerce the concept(s) into normal thinking patterns. With pure thought, this need is simply irrelevant since the limitations of thought do not apply when expressing the concept(s) in this manner.

Perception in these states is via sensing rather than the senses themselves, although they do sometimes play a key role as well. Spirit's (Óðr) strength is in pure sensing in which you perceive by sensing directly rather than via the physical senses. Typically, when developing sensing beyond the limits of the physical most people will start to instinctively develop the ability to sense from energy directly. It is a far more natural and normal way for the human being to sense, but has been relegated to the dormant parts of the mind for generations due to the overwhelming reliance on physical sensory input. The underlying information and knowledge contained within energy as it flows through Creation is both essential and phenomenal. By sensing this energy, one can also sense all of its characteristics including the information it carries. On the down side, one can also sense all the junk being broadcast via radio waves here, too. Because these waves are artificial, our natural sensing abilities do not pick them up as information. Instead, the radio waves act as disruptors to our perception. Unfortunately, we just have to work through this but the more you delve into deeper states of mind, the more skilful you will become in doing so. In the beginning, do not worry too much about extracting information from what you sense. It takes a little practice to get your brain to click into doing so. We will look at practices to develop pure thought and enhanced sensing in the sections below.

Deeper and Deeper: The Catapulting Trance Dance

This practice is built on a little trick of the brain-mind (Hugr) interactions and allows you, once mastered, to enter into incredibly deep trance states, the like of which people typically spend entire lifetimes chasing.

Simply enter a slight trance. You can use the typical "relax and let the world fade" trick for this. As soon as you feel the state of awareness deepen, break out of it and interrupt it. Count a few seconds (ideally about 5 or 6, see what works best for you) with your eyes open as if you were back in the typical standard state of awareness. Then immediately go back into the relaxation trick. Repeat this cycle one more time.

Next, perform the 'silencing the thoughts' technique outlined in the last exercise. As your trance deepens, break it again. Count 15-25 seconds with your eyes open before going back into trance via the 'silencing the thoughts' technique. When you renter the trance, you will notice it is much, much deeper. Then break it again and repeat the cycle once more (hence completing a threefold cycle).

If you have not worked with High Galdr yet simply stay in the trance you have achieved at the end of this and skip the rune energy stage given below. You will be able to do it later, for now build that trance entry skill set.

If you have already worked through your initial High Galdr learning, you can use it now to enhance this practice as follows: when you are about to break the cycle for the third time, you will use the energy of the ᛇ Jór (Eihwaz) rune to re-enter at that point. Instead of just re-entering trance as above, mentally (not vocally) chant the rune ᛇ Jór (Eihwaz) using High Galdr and pull the energy of the rune from about you into the spirit (Óðr). This will catapult you into the deepest trance you can imagine. Then break it and repeat for a total of two breaks. On the third, pull in all the energy of the rune into the spirit (Óðr) and stay in trance to do whatever you want to do within your trance state.

Quick Steps

1. Sit down and take a deep breath. Relax allow the world around you to fade.
2. As soon you have done so, you should be in a light trance state. Interrupt it.
3. Open your eyes and count to 5 or 6.
4. Immediately go back into the "relax and allow the world to fade away" technique, deepening your awareness once more.
5. Repeat steps 1-4 three times. You should notice by the third time that you are entering into a much deeper trance.
6. Like above, break the trance, open your eyes and shift out of it.
7. 5 or 6 seconds later go back into the relaxed state and do step 6 again.
8. Repeat steps 6-8 three times. You will notice that you are in an unusually strong and deep trance!

If you have learnt your High Galdr following these quick steps instead:

1. Sit down and take a deep breath. Relax and allow the world around you to fade.
2. As soon you have done so, you should be

in a light trance state. Interrupt it.

3. Open your eyes and count to 5 or 6.
4. Immediately go back into the "relax and allow the world to fade away" technique, deepening your awareness once more.
5. Repeat steps 1-4 three times. You should notice by the third time that you are entering into a much deeper trance.
6. If you have worked with High Galdr, use the ⟨ Jór (Eihwaz) rune, chant it (mentally only) and pull the energy it releases around you into your spirit (Óðr). This will deepen your trance substantially.
7. Like above, break the trance, open your eyes and shift out of it.
8. 5 or 6 seconds later go back into the relaxed state and do step 6 again.
9. Repeat steps 6-8 three times. You will notice that you are in an unusually strong and deep trance!

IN-BODY HUGR AND THE CONSCIOUS MIND

This title is going to confuse quite a few readers. You might be thinking is not consciousness in the body what we already have? The answer is both yes and no. What the title of this section is referring to is full consciousness within the body.

At best, most people are aware of the body only to a very limited degree, usually only when there is a need to move or do something — and even that is mostly automatic. Consciousness is focussed in the head region and on the hands and sometimes feet. The rest of the time, very little conscious action is put towards the body. For instance, are you aware of the individual muscles moving as you walk down the street? Are you aware of your spine as you walk? Sit? Move? Are you aware how your hair strands move in the wind? How your nostrils widen ever so slightly as you breathe? Very few people are.

Those who are aware of these things, however, are fully present in the here and now. Everyone else is on autopilot, their minds busy with imagining, planning, worrying and so forth. In order to achieve full body consciousness, this has to stop for two main reasons.

The first reason is that there is no body-mind unity in those instances. The more body-mind unity you have, the more information flows and the easier it becomes to reach the energy body (see below). How do you expect to achieve that when you are not even connected properly to your physical body? The second reason is that you are not grounded properly. This reason is even more important than the first. Proper grounding allows you to channel and pull more and more parts of the Self through the physical. You might wonder why bother with that? The answer is so simple, it evades many: your physical body is the receptacle and vehicle through which all parts of the Self are not only attached and inter-connected but through which they eventually achieve union. This needs to be achieved prior to death, otherwise you will have lost your chance and union is something the next generation will have to achieve.

Let us now look at the actual practice which, assuming you have mastered setting the Hugr Raven to Flight from 'The Spirit of Húnir Awakens (Part 1)', is very simple. Complete that exercise up to the point where your awareness is in the Hugr Raven in flight. Fly either to the heart level (if you are a biological female) or just above the genitals (if you are a biological male). Dive into the flesh. As you do this, feel, see and experience the Hugr Raven spilling from that point outwards through the entire body, not only the surface but the organs within, the muscles, the skeletal system, the blood system and so forth. Keep on dissolving throughout your body but do not merge with it. Simply allow the Raven to reshape its energy and allow that energy to flood each and every cell, nook and cranny of your body.

Now, just sit quietly and experience. This is a direct flooding of the mind and conscious awareness into the very cells of your physical being. Listen to your body; feel your body; experience your body. Harmonise with it and allow it to reach out to your mind. Allow it to be in the driving seat for the time being. Once you are familiar with this state of mind, reach out to an inch or so beyond your skin and allow the body's energy to provide you with information about your immediate environment. Let it whisper to you the deeper physiological realities it perceives which your mind is usually too busy and distracted to notice. Stay still and listen.

Next, open your eyes and fixate on something. Do not stare at the object or person but just observe passively. You will notice a thin band of energy, typically white or with a slight bluish tint. This is physical

Megin. Not to be confused with the energy body (Hamr), it is the energetic side of physical reality that your physical body (Lik) is picking up. Remember when using this type of energetic vision, it is all about seeing the energy around things. This will also help you distinguish between what is illusory and what is real. Illusory or imagined objects do not emit energy. The same runs true for all things in Creation.

When done, refocus on the body and pull back all the (mind) Hugr energy spread throughout your physical form. Condense it, pulling it all back into the area at which you entered with it. Eventually, it will reshape to the usual Raven form. When it does, push out and fly to the front of your physical body once more. To end the practice, follow the typical ending described in the "Setting the Hugr Raven to Flight" exercise.

Quick Steps

1. Start by doing the Setting the Hugr Raven to Flight found in Part 1.
2. With your awareness within the Hugr raven, float down to the level of the heart (if you are a biological female) or just above the genitals (if you are a biological male).
3. From that point, drive inwards. Diving into the flesh, feel the Raven form flooding inwards throughout the entire physical body (Lik), spilling through the bones, muscles, blood, nerves so forth. Feel it spilling throughout the DNA in each and every one of your cells.
4. Do not allow yourself to merge with the

body. You must keep the perspective of the observer. This separation of awareness from the physical body (Lik) whilst flowing through it is essential.

5. Experience your body from this point of view as long as possible.

6. Feel at one with it, with each and every cell of your physical being.

7. Reach out to it and allow its own conscious-ness to reach out to your mind.

8. When you have acquired this perception, expand about one inch or so outwards from the physical body into the energy field around it.

9. Listen to what it communicates to you from those things your mind typically does not pay attention to or is simply too distracted to. Stay still listen and sense it. Allow what-ever information surfaces to flow into your awareness.

10. Open your physical eyes. Remember to keep your awareness separate from them. What you should keep in mind is that you are seeing through the Hugr. It is the Hugr which is looking through the physical eyes. Whatever you notice from the physical eyes is simply a by-product of the Hugr sending you that perception rather than you seeing through them directly.

11. Fixate on something. It could be an object, your hand, anything. Keep your eyes focussed at its centre. Relax the eyes and be aware

of what is happening in the peripheral view.

12. You should see a thin band of white or slightly bluish energy. If you are looking at a body part or person, this is megin flowing through the body. If you are looking at an object, it is pure energy.

13. When done, refocus on your physical body and the feeling and sensation of the cells within but this time, start pulling all that Hugr raven energy back out of it.

14. Pool it all at the point where you entered and reform the raven. Exit the physical form of your body.

15. Fly out and end your practice as you learnt to do in the Setting the Hugr Raven to Flight exercise.

This is an important practice for you to master. It will stretch the mental perceptions of our physical reality. Not only that but you will start to develop your six senses to a whole new level and prepare them for purer energetic sensing. Using this practice, you are in effect dancing on the line in-between physical energy and pure energy. Another important skill set this yields is the ability to communicate and understand your physical body (Lik). After practicing for a while, you instantly know when something is wrong even before health issues start to develop. Instinctively, you will begin to keep away from foods, drinks and anything else which your biological intelligence considers harmful. You will also learn to not only experience other peoples' bodies that you make contact with but also how to share information with them biologically from nervous system to nervous system. Additionally, you are learning to perceive energy directly by teaching the physical body how the mind perceives and learning how the body perceives without the interference of your mind. We will cover this in much more depth at a later point in time.

BODY (LIK) – MIND (ÓÐR-HUGR) TRICK

We are not going to delve too much into the relationships and interactions of the various parts of the Self at this stage. Those are best studied in the light of runic experiencing and will be covered at a later time. For now, however, it is important to mention one such interaction which will make the work at hand so much easier.

The trick involves stillness of the body. As we will see, the body, the mind and the spirit are intrinsically interlinked, affecting one another on a constant basis. Because the body and energy body are interlinked in a very similar fashion, the flow of influence is as follows: mind (Óðr-Hugr) -> body (Lik) -> energy body (Hamr). The mind does not have direct influence on the energy body. Instead, it gains that influence via the medium of the physical body. This is why, in so many cases, the energy body can be at odds with the mind and they have such a hard time communicating with one another. Most people never experience their communication at all. That is the default modus operandi of the human Self. But when we still the body,

25

it automatically starts to still the mind due to this interconnectivity.

To practice this technique, find a chair with back support which will ensure that your back is kept straight and does not curve as it would on a sofa. Your legs should be kept parallel with feet on the floor. If you can feel the floor, so much the better. Do not use any Eastern cross-legged positions! Those are not ideal for either our physiology nor our energy systems, as people from the West and the East have different energy systems and physiological adaptations. Finally, place your hands on your thighs, (left hand on the left leg, right hand on the right leg). Sit still — no movement is allowed. Just keep in perfect stillness. At first, it will be hard due to lack of discipline and doing something new but, with a little practice, it will become second nature. The body, being smarter than the mind, adapts very rapidly.

Once you have gained the ability to sit in stillness, combine it with the "Silencing the Mind" techniques above, especially the trance dance. You will be able to observe how much faster the thought process slows down and how effectively you can enter into trance states.

RUNES FOR THOUGHT STILLNESS

You might be wondering why we are not using runes during these. The reasons are twofold. First, using runic energy to achieve this new default mind state is not advisable. Why? Because if you do, you will be introducing runic energy into your working which with later techniques might be incompatible. For instance, if you use the ᚠ Óss (Ansuz) rune to enter trance for the purpose of travelling in your Fylgja, Minni or Hamr, it disrupts the separation process of those parts of the Self (although it works wonders as far as the Hugr Raven is concerned). If you are entering trance to manipulate fire rune energy, adding an air rune can make the whole accumulation blow up on you. Relying on a rune to enter into altered mind states is never a good idea because it can contaminate the work for which you are going into trance. So buckle up, ladies and gents! Work at your trance and stillness using only your mind and sheer persistent effort.

The other reason we are avoiding using runic energy to still the mind is that many people dabbling into runic energy will misguidedly use the ᛁ Íss (Isa) rune's energy to still the flow of thought in their minds. While it will have the desired effect, introducing the primal ice current into the mind will also slow down the intellect, solidify memory towards stasis and 'freeze' the mental parts of the Self. In effect, you are locking yourself down. The frost runes are very difficult to use and extremely dangerous even when mastered. Their effects often go unnoticed due to the fact that, in Midgard, it will be gradual slowing. If you slow down the mind just a little, you will seldom notice this, unless you are deeply in-tune with it. Each time, however, you slow it down more and more. By the time you notice that your intellect has decreased, that you cannot speed up trance states and your general degradation of capacity, the damage has already been done. Never leave ᛁ Íss (Isa) energy floating about unless you are planning on using it against something.

27

RECLAIMING THE MIND
&
ENERGETIC SELF

Unlocking the Limitations of Thought

As you spend more and more time in a thoughtless state, you will notice many changes taking place. Your mind will be harder for other people or things to distract. Suggestions and hypnosis will become less and less effective. The ability to penetrate a concept, idea or question and to think in terms of abstractions will be greatly amplified. Most importantly, you will start to acquire knowledge instantly and answers will spontaneously come to mind. While other people will have to think hard, work out solutions and plan, you will just know instead. It is critically important to maintain a type of behaviour which suggests you still do those things or otherwise it will terrify those around you.

Your observation skills will be so amplified that all you will need is a single glance and you will penetrate deep into whatever you are observing. When observing other people, you will literally penetrate their very Self. Your gaze will go into the deepest layers of their very beings. This can be, and often is, very disconcerting to others as their energy bodies will feel it but they will not be able to interpret what it is they felt. You can lessen these effects by focussing on interacting with their physical bodies rather than their minds. Unfortunately, no matter what you do, it is impossible not to interact with their energies. That comes as a natural consequence of becoming aware of energy in its various states. Just make sure the knowledge you gain is kept private — a form of respect is the basis of our social interaction at the energetic level of reality and what you are doing is exercising direct perception of the world about you. We will look at how this can be enhanced to an even greater degree but for now, suffice it to learn about it and start experiencing it.

Again we will be using no runes to enhance its effects. There are a few combinations one could employ but we will leave those for later on in the advanced practices below. By doing the work on the Óðrerir (see 'Óðrerir: The Norse 'Holy Grail' in the advanced section) and Setting the Hugr Raven to Flight[5], these abilities will be naturally enhanced even before we start throwing runic power at them.

By unlocking the mind past the limitations of thought, what you are actually achieving is a higher form of mental function. This is the borderline of human thought function and spirit thoughtless function. In many traditions, we find mention of lower and higher parts of the mental levels of reality. However, there are simply no such things. There is only one mental level and it is how we function within it that builds the illusion of it having layers. By increasing your type of mental function, you are able to touch and eventually step over into purer and more abstract manifestations on the mental level. This is why you also experience the widening in scope of perception and mental capabilities and why the limitations imposed by thought hold back our spiritual development, subjecting us to illusions, deceptions and mis-directions.

THE 'MIND THIEF'

You may not know this but our minds are under assault. As a result of this, our perceptual capabilities are kept at their lowest possible level.

This assault is carried out by what can be called the 'Mind Thief', an energetic predatory organism very much like the familiar virus but with a form of intelligence of its own. Understanding the 'Mind Thief' is not really necessary. Trying to do so is really nothing more than a distraction. However, understanding what it does and how it does it is very important.

Have you ever wondered why you suddenly have countless thoughts, problems, issues and so forth bubbling up into your mind out of nowhere as soon as you try to calm down and enter into the relaxed state of focus? Or that when you need to focus properly, waves upon waves of distractions pop up? Science would tell you it is just the brain's neurological system firing up thoughts at random because that is what it does. However, this is both correct and incorrect. Such things are effects of the brain's neurons firing but something is causing them to fire in the first place. Those who see energy will know full well that what is causing this firing and making your mind a real chatterbox anytime you try to silence it and gain control. For our purposes, we will call it the 'Mind Thief'. This thief has only one goal: energy. It is mainly here to gather as much of your energy and memories as it can during your lifetime. When you die, it leaves your body fully charged and carrying extra pieces back to where it came from originally until it finds a new host.

One thing that these mind thieves cannot stand is silence, stillness and control. They need the constant activity, the constant generations of thoughts and thought-waves to both feed and act as a reference point. Think of the human mind as a receiving and broadcasting radio device. Going silent is very disturbing allowing the channel to be tuned into anything useful is even more disturbing to these 'listeners'. Why? If your energy is focused onto actual purposes rather than random mind-chatter, then they cannot harvest it. Worry, fears, imagined scenarios, imagined dangers, idle fantasising all generate energy but since it is undirected and has no intent or purpose behind it, it creates the ideal feeding ground for these parasites.

They attach to us on the energetic level mentally at first but since the human being uses all three of the mental parts of the Self rather actively, they will descend via the energy systems to sit in the Hamr. Because the Hamr is totally unused by most humans at this stage of awareness, it makes a good base for it to hide. The 'Mind Thief' can then hijack that connection to the active part of the mind (Hugr) and to the shadow (Sal). It will engineer both mental and physiological reactions, responses and instigator events for them purely to gather energy. As it sits in the Hamr, it is in direct receipt of all the energy generated by and circulated through the energy body. There will be more on this in the relevant teachings.

Since we are dealing with the mind, let us focus on the mental side of this 'thief'. From its position in the Self, it will interject impulses into the Hugr which are typically nudges towards activity. This also gives it a solid connection to the Minni. It then pulls nice juicy memories out of the Minni to which it knows you will react, prods the Hugr into activity and keeps prodding. As far as it is concerned, the problem is now fixed. Your mind is distracted by pointless contemplations, worries and all sorts of imagined planning and scenarios. Smart, is it not? All this activity results in a whole range of energy expenditure via thought. If it can start a chain reaction with something you are going to be angry or feel frustrated about, all the better — it will collect the emotional charges as they flow from the energy body (Hamr) and feed off the shadow (Sal) while reaping the thought-generated energetic charges as they flow from Minni to Hugr.

All this activity ultimately leads to mental fatigue because energising thought requires a large amount of energy. It is also by default one of the highest vibrating energies that any individual can produce. Typically, most people will not notice this fatigue until it fully hits them. Some will be able to notice a slowing down of their speed of processing mentally, while others will experience more and more difficulty in thinking 'straight' as it is termed. Still others will experience a loss of clarity in their thinking. Now, let us be fair and recognise, too, that this can be due to the brain's lack of nourishment (mainly glucose) but, provided there are no brain disorders present, even that could well be a side effect of these underlying occurrences.

How do you catch it & What happens To It at death?

The 'Mind Thief' is transmitted the same way as all viral things are. This being an energetic thing, however, it does not suffer from the same limitation that a biological virus would have. In this case, contact or proximity to anyone else with infected with one will automatically cause a transference. Since it is present in almost all humans at this point in time, infection happens quite soon after birth as the child has then lost the protection of the mother's energy body.

This might seem like a doom and gloom situation but there are very simple ways of purging it. In addition, by strengthening one's own protections, it is more than possible to keep these things at bay. For those who do not, these mind thieves will stay with them until death. At that point they will start to disassociate themselves from the person in whom they have lived. Frequently, because most people have lived their entire lives with the thief, a type of symbiotic joining happens which is difficult to separate from. As such, the consciousness of the person after death is carried with the escaping thief until it reaches its destination and totally detaches. That is why many people report travelling down a tunnel with a light at the end during near death experiences. Others report similarly wonderful experiences which are often dream-like but so vivid that they seem even more real than our own reality. These are all merely energetic patterns carried by the thief as it departs the deceased Self.

Once this disconnect from the 'Mind Thief' happens, consciousness loses its cohesion and is unable to continue on its own for long due to having very limited resources. We will look at the psycho-spiritual dynamics of death in more detail at a later stage.

WHY GET RID OF THE 'MIND THIEF'?

It seems strange but most people would ask why would you want to get rid of it? After all, it has been with them since birth so why does it matter?

The first reason is simple: unless we stop this thief from stripping us of what limited energy resources we have available, progress on an energetic and spiritual level becomes impossible. Our bodies can only hold a limited amount of energy and that is all you have available to work with. Vast amounts of this energy are already used to maintain conscious awareness and even more is needed to fuel perception itself. Just perceiving and interacting with the world in our daily lives consumes almost all of our resources, hence even a tiny excess of energy loss is extremely damaging. In 'The Breath of Oðin Awakens'[6], we saw how to start replenishing the megin but now it is time to learn how to both reclaim the mental side of our energy and increase it, too.

Second, our minds were never naturally made to be subject to constant waves upon waves of chatter and activation. It is an energetic interference just like all the radio waves that bombard us on a constant basis. These interferences block us off from the focussed mind states which are required for trance and connecting to the spirit (Óðr), as well as perceptions of non-typical events (including energy perceptions). Once you establish a clearer mind, everything else is easier to deal with. Illusions are easier to cut through, stillness is easier to obtain, balance of the entire Self is more readily available and, most importantly, control of one's own mind is possible. Achieving that control then allows you to start controlling and manipulating energy, which in turn enables proper mastery of the runes and runic streams. Without control, there can be no actual results and it starts in one's own Self.

Finally, once removed, spare energy is no longer wasted on the mind thief. Instead, it now flows freely to the shadow (Sal) in order to fuel the hatching of the energy body (Hamr) itself.

HOW TO GET RID OF THE 'MIND THIEF'?

This is accomplished in three main phases. First off, you will need to establish a state of silence of the mind — not an emptiness of thought but freedom from the chitter-chatter (broadcasting) of the mind and other internal or external distractions.

You will need to obtain six clear quartz crystals about 2 inches or so in height. The small pillar types are best for this. Larger is okay but do not go under 2 inches.

Next, sit down and make sure there are no distractions about. Turn off your mobile phone or place them in another room. Turn off the television and radio. The same goes for computers, tablets and so forth. Remove everything which can distract.

Place the three crystals between your fingers of the right hand and another three in between the fingers of the left hand. You want to have one in between the index and middle finger, one between middle and ring finger and finally one between the ring finger and small one. If they are pillar types, having the points downwards will make them fit nicely into the curvature of the fingers. Place the hand on the legs and let it rest, making sure the crystals do not fall out. Place the other hand on the leg for comfort too.

Relax. Close your eyes and breathe comfortably. Look straight ahead in the darkness behind your closed eyelids. Do not imagine or try and see anything. Ignore all that for now and just relax, keeping the eyes focussed straight ahead. When a thought pops up, observe it and allow it to pass. Try to keep the mind as free of thought as possible. When one pops in just let it pass and avoid focusing in on it.

You will notice that, when using the crystals, thoughts may pop up at first but it's not too often. When they do, it takes practically no effort to be avoid being carried away by a train of thought. All you need to do is use your fingers to initiate pressure against the crystals and it will short circuit the onslaught of thoughts. You will also notice that you have silence or a stillness of the mind between thoughts. Just make note of it and keep at the practice. You will be jumping over thoughts from moment of stillness to moment of stillness. The more you do this, the longer those moments will last. This is the goal of the practice.

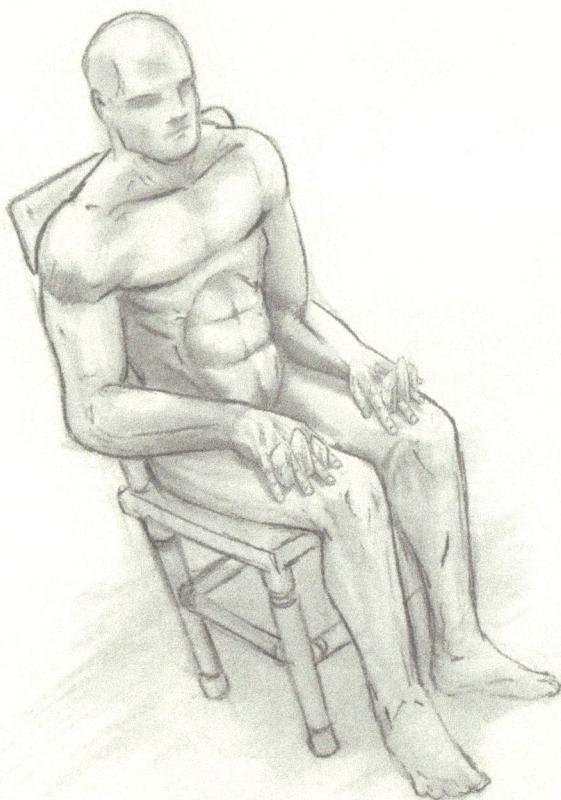

Countering the 'Mind Thief'
Practice Position (with crystals)

Quick Steps

1. Obtain 6 quartz crystals, about 2 inches in height each.
2. Sit down or lie down and ensure no distractions will be able to disturb your practice.
3. Place a crystal in-between your index and middle finger, another in-between the middle and ring finger and the final one in-between the ring finger and little finger. Repeat with the other hand. Rest both hands in a comfortable position.
4. Relax and breathe comfortably, allowing the world to fade from your immediate awareness.
5. As in the Silencing of the Mind practice, close your eyes and focus them straight ahead.
6. Relax and observe your thoughts.
7. This time you are going to try and keep the mind empty of thought. Each time a thought pops up squeeze the crystals and focus on the pain or pressure it causes as the middle joints of the fingers.
8. You will notice that the pain caused breaks the flow of thoughts and helps re-establish the silence more and more.

A few things to note: as you do this, you might notice your body going tense and trying to shift. Ignore it and simply relax through it. At other times, you might also get a sense of panic. Ignore this, too. These are all signals that the 'Mind Thief' is in crisis.

This is EXACTLY what we want. Since it is energetic and connected to the body, it will try and force you to move or disrupt your practice. This is normal, too. Just ignore it and keep relaxing through its shenanigans. It will also try to spur more and more thoughts. Just relax through that, too, and let go of them. Enjoy the moments of stillness and relax.

Another thing you might notice is that the crystals are making pressure on bones of the fingers. This is what we want because that pressure will help you maintain focus as well as interrupt the energy flow in between the fingers (we will look at the finger-mind connection at a later point in time).

If you do this practice for quite a while, you could notice the crystals getting warm even though your fingers do not give off enough heat to do so. If this happens, you are doing things right. They are capturing the energy which would have gone straight to the 'Mind Thief'. This is the energy that it forces your system to generate for its consumption.

To put this another way, we are achieving here quite a few things in this exercise. Firstly, we are developing your ability to still the Hugr and Minni (your mind), enhancing control of the mental level of your Self, causing panic in the 'Mind thief' and stripping it of its energy which, in turn, will weaken it over the course of time. Basically, we are changing our Self's environment to become incredibly hostile to this invader and stripping it of resources, which we are then holding onto for our own use. If you are going to be practicing runic dream-walking, which will be covered at a future point in time, save these charged crystals for the practices outlined in there.

This stillness of mind will in and of itself expand your perceptive awareness, allowing you to enter into very deep states of trance and begin to establish your connection with your own spirit (Óðr).

Repeat this practice as many times as you can. It is preferable to do it on a daily basis. The benefits you gain will rapidly become noticeable. Always seek to deepen the periods in which you achieve stillness of the mind. This is the crux of the matter at hand and is of vital importance to everything later on. Without the ability to still the mind, you will not be able to enter into deeper trances or expand your mental capabilities much beyond those of daily life. As you get into the habit, you will also notice that it is easier to get into this stillness and that the amount of disturbances you encounter are reduced. This means your mental functions are returning to their normal and natural state. Keep up the good work! Make your mind so inhospitable that it kills off the 'Mind Thief' and takes you off their map.

RUNIC PRACTICES TO COUNTER THE 'MIND THIEF'

Countering the mind thief is pretty much an ongoing task until it is finally neutralised and can no longer return. Our practices with stilling the mind will help tremendously but we are by no means going to leave it at that. An invader has taken over and it is time we 'debug' the darn thing.

In order to understand what is being done, we

have to make a bit of a jump into the next level of the Self, namely the energetic. At the energetic level of the Self we will find the physical body (Lik) sitting at its apex. For the time being, all we need to be aware of is that the 'Mind Thief' rests within the energetic makeup of the physical body. It is, after all, an infection which has settled from the mental into the physical and gained energetic dimensionality.

The runes to be used are quite complex and include I Íss (Isa), M Eykur (Ehwaz), M Maður (Mannaz), S Sól (Sowilo), ↑ Jór (Eihwaz), Þ Þurs (Thurisaz) and ♦ Ár (Jera). Ideally, they would be combined into a bindrune and charged using High Galdr methods. For now, however, we will reserve the discussion of that advanced practice for a later time and instead do this manually. We will return to the actual bindrune in due course.

The process itself involves re-establishing the Will at the root of the Self (S Sól (Sowilo)), then expanding through to the level of the 'Mind Thief' (↑ Jór (Eihwaz)), forcing it into stasis (I Íss (Isa)), reversing its evolution (♦ Ár (Jera)) which will devolve it to the point where it can be destroyed (Þ Þurs (Thurisaz)). Then we re-harmonise (M Eykur (Ehwaz)) the various parts of the Self which will have been thrown off balance by our destroying something (the 'Mind Thief') it had become used to seeing as yet another part of itself. Finally, we will re-establish the fully functional Self (M Maður (Mannaz)). Job done!

In order to do this, go into as deep a trance as you can. If you are sufficiently practised at it, you may use the trance dance technique, if you so desire. Chant the S Sól (Sowilo) rune, pulling its energy into your physical body (Lik) and spirit (Óðr). Will your actual Self to be strengthened and break through any bindings or illusions at play. ⚡ Sól (Sowilo) has a light energy that can be visualised as a shining white laser beam which cuts through everything. Then use the ᛇ Jór (Eihwaz) rune visualised in the traditional red energy. ᛇ Jór (Eihwaz)'s energy penetrates everything, flowing throughout all realities. As it does, will it to shift your awareness directly to the 'Mind Thief' within. A note of warning: absolutely avoid thinking of it on a universal scale! First you will need to fix your Self before you go for any big battles!

When ready, focus on the 'Mind Thief'. It sits in the energetic centre of the physical body (Lik) at the top of the head (also called the crown centre) and expands downwards into and through the body's nervous system. For those who can see energy it will look very much like an inverted partial egg shape emitting a pendulum type of energy swinging from the left to the right and vice versa. You are going to have to keep your focus on it at all times. Remember the warnings given about using the rune ᛁ Íss (Isa) to still the mind above? Those same warnings apply to all the runes. We want to be very specific at what we are striking. The 'Mind Thief' can be felt as a left-right-left-right pendulum type of energy. If you have entered a deep enough trance, you will sense it immediately. That energy is its core and that is what we are going to be striking with all you have. But rather than just bashing at it, we are doing a precise surgeon's strike.

Use the black icy energy of ᛁ Íss (Isa), directing it to the 'Mind Thief' above your head. Will it to impose

47

the icy stasis of Creation within its very core. This will render it unable to react and temporarily freeze its energies and activity. You will feel a sudden release of mental tension but do not allow it to distract you. Chant the ᛃ Ár (Jera) rune but, rather than using its typical colour, you will visualise it in a dark, almost damp yellow. Feel its heavy, moist energy as you fling it into the 'Mind Thief's core, willing it to reverse its evolution and keep at it. Make the energy spin anti-clockwise — this has the effect of condensing it, making its reach lesser and lesser but also making it denser. We need that effect for the next strike. As it condenses, it will pull back into its core all the pieces of itself that it had tendrilled through you. Once you have it coiled up on itself, unleash as powerful a casting of ᚦ Þurs (Thurisaz) as you can muster. See and feel the electric spark shoot out at the now condensed and sluggish core of the 'Mind Thief'. The more violently you can do this, the better. As it hits, see it shatter and disperse until there are nothing more than energy particles floating away from you UNTIL YOU CAN SEE THEM NO LONGER!.

You will be buzzing a little from all of this but that is perfectly normal. If this was done right, you will feel as if a fog has been lifted from your mind. Some describe it as though a heaviness had been lifted. Whatever it is, you will feel a distinct sensation upon its departure. Before you do anything else, use the ᛖ Eykur (Ehwaz) rune to re-harmonise your Self. Feel its solid white energy flow through you. Feel the protective and harmonising sensations that it carries within each and every part of your Self. Will them all to be in perfect harmony with each other and with your conscious awareness. Finally, use the ᛗ Maður (Mannaz) rune, feeling its soft comforting gentle airy red touch surround you and flow through and about you. At this point, you should feel unity and balance within all parts of your Self.

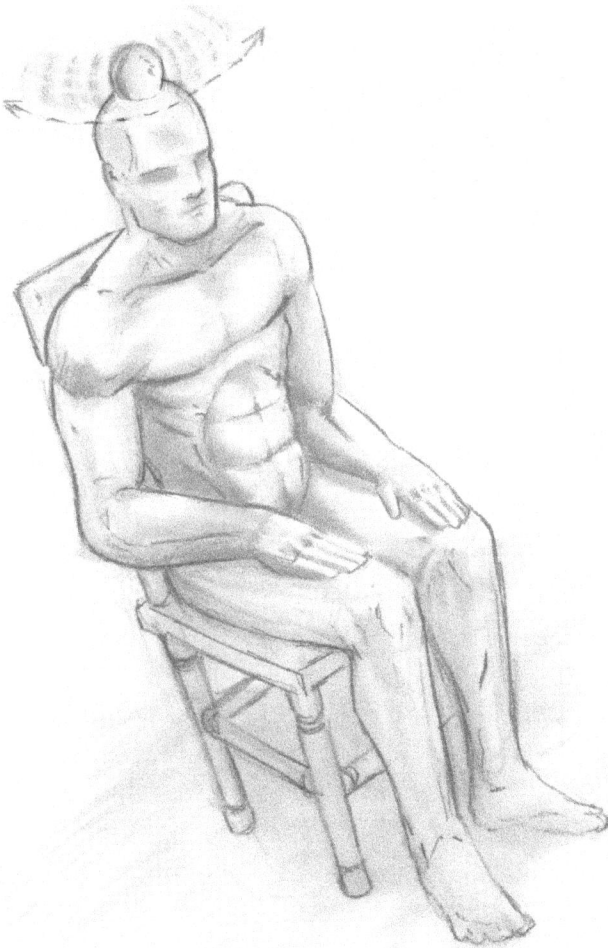

'Mind Thief' Location
in Human Beings'

Quick Steps

1. Go into as deep a trance as possible.

2. Use trance dance if you have mastered it.

3. Chant the rune ⚡ Sól (Sowilo) (or use High Galdr for it), pulling its energy into the physical body (Lik) and the spirit (Óðr). Will it to stren-gthen the Self and break through any bindings or illusions that it is under.

4. Next, use ⟍ Jór (Eihwaz) rune in the trad-itional red energy colour. Intend it to shift your awareness and gain focus of the 'Mind Thief' within. This will deepen the trance more.

5. When your focus has shifted, you will be able to lock into the sense of the core of the 'Mind Thief' at the top of your head like an inverted partial egg shape.

6. Chant I Íss (Isa) and direct its black icy energy into the core of the inverted egg shape. This will freeze its core but only temporarily. Do not allow anything to distract you.

7. Chant the rune ♦ Ár (Jera) (or use High Galdr), visualising its heavy dark yellow energy spin-ning anti-clockwise around the core of the 'Mind Thief'. This will condense it and make it smaller. As it does, strike it with a powerful burst of ▶ Þurs (Thurisaz) runic energy.

8. As ▶ Þurs (Thurisaz) is chanted, see the lightning strikes hit the core of the 'Mind Thief' and shattering it into billions and billions of the tiniest particles possible. See

them flow into the emptiness of Creation all around you until they fade out completely.

9. Now chant the ᛗ Eykur (Ehwaz) rune unleashing its solid white energy to flow through you, intending it to harmonise your Self.

10. Finally chant the ᛗ Maður (Mannaz) rune, feeling its soft red airy energy flow through you and bringing with it harmony and unity through you and every part of your being.

In other runic workings, we would usually dismiss all of the energies used, but not in this case. We NEED this all to stick, so we will leave these energies to circulate and exercise their effects until they naturally dissipate on their own. If need be, feel free to repeat this until you feel the full release but once you have felt it, do not repeat it any more. There is no need and thinking of the 'Mind Thief' when it is not actually there will attract a new infection. If you would like to repeat the final two runes for a general re-harmonisation and balancing, feel free to do so any time you need it. That final part of the practice can be done with any issue whatsoever.

Secret functions of the rune ᛋ Sól (Sowilo)

This is a good place to mention a few words with respect to the ᛋ Sól (Sowilo) rune. As you will have noticed, its use is somewhat different than what you would typically expect it to be. This is because of its inherent functions on the archetypal level of Creation. We will look at this in much more detail when starting our practice of actual High Galdr but for now, it is important to start grasping the archetypal concepts of this runic energy.

ᛋ Sól (Sowilo) is the rune of manifestation of the Self on the archetypal level. It is directly linked to the Spark of the Self in its characteristics. It represents the separation of Self from the whole or, put in other terms, the springing forth of individualistic character-istics and properties from the Ginnungagap at the point of creation of the Spirit (Óðr) by Húnir. This out-pouring of the essence of the Self in all its glory and potential. It is the totality of the Self rushing towards realisation via manifestation but as of yet unrealised.

This was triggered by Oðin upon the gifting of the Meign-filled breath (Önd) to the first humans whilst they were still technically trees (Ash and Embla). It is not the luck of the draw that the ᛦ Ýr (Elhaz) rune (divine manifestation and influence) precedes the ᛋ Sól (Sowilo) one. Using ᛋ Sól (Sowilo) when we need to re-establish the actual individualistic parts of the essence of Self is one of the primary functions for this runic energy at the archetypal level of Creation and the Self. It flows counter-clockwise as the Self condenses and solidifies into the energetic physicality and then shifts into clockwise directionality as the Self spiritualises back into the spiritual carrying the physicality. We will be making use of these features of ᛋ Sól (Sowilo) quite extensively as we continue in our work on the realisation of the Self.

RECLAIMING THE ENERGETIC SELF

You will notice that energy is frequently mentioned in Norse Mysticism. This is because it forms part of the core reality of our very existence. So far, it has been looked at mostly in terms of external energy and the management of our own energy but it is now time to take a deeper look at our internal energy itself.

When discussing energy, the vast majority of humans think of it in terms of the known energy types that we interact with on a daily basis, such as electricity, heat, light, and so forth. Such reasoning is, in and of itself, highly limiting. When thinking of it in this manner, only a fraction of the nature of energy is grasped. No one can be blamed for this limitation of perception since we are all rigidly taught it and conditioned to perceive this way since childhood. This in turn limits our understanding of it, our scope of thinking in terms of it, as well as our conceptualisations of its possibilities. Well, it is time to start stretching our concepts of what energy is.

There is an important reality to energy which you will need to wrap your mind around: energy is conscious. Oh, the arguments that gives rise to! If you think of consciousness in terms of thinking, logic and so forth (in other words only in terms of the scope of the Hugr), you will get stuck. But as we know, the mental side of our very Self is not only the mind-reason (Hugr), that is only one of the secondary parts of it. The Spirit (Óðr) holds the key to this level of Self and energy has Spirit (Óðr). In other words, a type of spirit essence flows through all energy because it is part and parcel of all energy's very nature and constituent characteristics. Those who think along these lines will realise immediately that this Spirit (Óðr) and consciousness is very different from that which is part of our Self. In short, energy has consciousness which is different from that of a human being but is conscious nonetheless.

We need to be careful to avoid the human tendency of personalisation here. You see it everywhere. As soon as you mention that something is conscious and has spirit, the human mind immediately seeks to attach personality to it. Avoid this at all costs! Personality results from a very complex interplay of the Self as a whole, which is something other forms of consciousness do not possess. In those terms, we can think of general energy as having a very basic yet highly advanced non-personalised consciousness.

A little context might help with grasping this concept. The most common type of energy that everyone comes across is what we call life force, that mysterious energy which gives rise to life itself, maintains it and eventually leaves at death whereupon decay sets in. Life force has its own consciousness which

seeks to engender life and express its key characteristic which is, of course, life. This is why it is so
attracted to the human body. Our bodies have millions
if not billions of ways of expressing life. The consciousness of the life force energy will come into our bodies
and immediately seek to flow through it in order to
express LIFE. It does not care what part it flows through,
how it is used by it, whether there is too much of it
already there or not. All it does is express life through
a medium to which it is brilliantly suited. By doing
so, it boosts us in all manner of ways, some of which
we know and are aware and others that we never
even think of. Yet none of this matters to it. This is a
simple yet highly effective consciousness. It lacks
reason, it lacks deductions, it lacks perceptive abilities,
it lacks the ability to decide and so forth — all it
knows is that the human being is an ideal vehicle
through which it can express itself and it wants to
be 'expressed'.

As it flows through the human being, it shares in
him or her, experiences through them, is enriched and
given a specific vibration, a colour, an added richness
which it never could have gained on its own. It now
becomes personal life force. Just as it has contributed
to our life, we have contributed to its essence. And
so life force jumps from life form to life form, growing,
expanding and enriching itself yet still maintaining
that basic type of life consciousness.

It is by no means whatsoever limited to human
beings. It does this with any life form it can but it
will always flow most in those which have the greatest
potential of expressing life in the most diverse ways
possible. This is why all this move to human-machine

merge is actually highly limiting for us. By moving away from the biological to the synthetic, we would be limiting the versatility of potential of expression for the life force. Hence it would not only flow in lesser quantities through us but it would also see us as an inferior organism for expression of itself and move onto another more superior one.

By becoming part synthetic, we become less alive! Do not forget life force fuels our minds, our essences and each and every part of our Self! The whole concept that we will be smarter and have greater intellectual capabilities if we merge with technology is just a big fallacy. If you are less alive, you are less conscious, less aware and perceive less. What is worse in terms of synthetic interference with life is that it would control the extent of the perceptions one is capable of, rather than our Self doing so.

The same principle which applies to the drives and types of consciousness that life force has runs true in other energies, albeit they have slightly different foci and scope which will match their underlying characteristics. Creation sees sameness as a waste of resource which it then tries to eliminate. At the same time, it loves uniqueness which it protects and promotes.

The same runs true for the energy which we produce. It is an amalgamation of all the energies which come into us with a tint of what we ourselves contribute to it, combined with the underlying essence of our Self which gives us a unique individualised energy. Seeing as our consciousness and experiences are so vast on so many different levels of awareness (whether we are conscious of it or not), it produces a fascinating type of energy. Due to the constant perceptual activity of our being, it is constantly in flux and makes something which could be compared to the ripples you see when you throw a stone into a pool of water. The more activity, the faster it will ripple, but ripple it will. This will be discussed in more depth when looking at the energy body below.

The important part of the discussion at this point in time is that it carries our essence, a part of us. This might be a very strange concept to many of you and a very familiar one to others. In order to work from a common basis of understanding, let us take a closer look at this.

Our energy, like practically all others in existence, carries this fundamental consciousness which all energy has. It is conscious but since it is generated at higher levels of reality or rather complexities of conscious-ness, it possesses far greater degrees of consciousness and breadth than simpler ones. What this means is that it will carry a tint (or hue) of the Self of that person, the information they are privy to and a degree of their consciousness which an energy such as the raw life force does not have. We are, in actuality, energy beings which have solidified into bodies but are nonetheless still energy beings. As such, when we exchange energies, touch energies, or give some of our energy away, we are exchanging, touching and giving a tiny part of ourselves. This forms a type of relationship where we flow through whatever we exchanged with and it in turns flows through us.

This matters for a number of reasons. For one, as mentioned earlier, the amount of energy to which you have access is always limited. It is limited in part to the total amount you can hold in your Self, by how much flows through you and by how much you use. The same principle holds true for Megin. Use it up and you run out. As long as you are alive, you will regenerate it but you cannot automatically regenerate more than your current level. Think about all the things you do on a daily basis, the ridiculous amounts of energy our awareness takes, that our senses need to function, that our minds need, our daily activities take, our bodies need and so forth. This all stretches our total available energy to its very limit. If you follow this train of thought, you will see that one of the main reasons that there is no energy left for additional non-physical activities is simply because we typically use up all the available pools of energy we have for daily life. In addition to this, the more of it you share with others, the more it in turn reduces the total available pool.

Following this line of thinking, you could be left wondering, 'but what of all the energy we produce from food?' Eating does indeed generate massive amounts of energy but that energy is mainly used to sustain our bodies. The reason for this is simply due to the fact that the foods we eat produce a very dense form of energy which can only fuel the lowest parts of the Self. Even at that level, we have a total lack of fuelling of the Sal and only partial fuelling of the Hamr. The rest of the Self is left with no nutrition from food itself. Remember the 'you are what you eat' principle? It applies all too well to our Self. We eat physical food and end up being bound to this physicality. Having said all this, some foods do result in higher than 'standard' energy types and can effect the other parts of the Self. A most notable example of this are herbs and drugs, which in some cases can have rather impressive and / or devastating effects when not consumed properly.

RECLAIMING YOUR ENERGY

In order to enable us to use our own energy as we please, we need to start by reclaiming it. This is simply an extension of the above because when we leave our energy or give it away, we are also losing that part of ourselves over the course of a lifetime. This thinning out of the Self reaches a point where only a sliver of it is left. This is one of the reasons why people complain of becoming tired of life as they age. It is not the ageing but the loss of Self and its potential as well as totality of energy which is diminishing all capabilities and potential of expression and perception of the Self — not a desirable state of affairs by any stretch of the imagination.

Each time you meet a person, you experience something in life, whether it is building a memory or feeling a burst of emotion, you are throwing out some of your energy and locking it into that event. Because we are, technically speaking, expelling energy this creates a vacuum which needs to be filled. Think of it as a small hole which is empty. Nothing stays empty per se, so this hole then fills with energy from either that other person, the environment or whatever energy was directed at you. In effect, this creates a big problem because you are being forced to exchange your own energy for what is essentially an alien energy. The more different this is from your own, the bigger the issues you will experience and the more of an exchange which takes place, the greater the weakening of the Self.

This universal mechanism is very interesting when looking at deliberate energy exchanges such as during sex, forceful evolution and development which is outside of the scope of a person's natural capabilities. Those will be dealt with in great detail at a later time.

The arrogant many will immediately think well 'I can transform that energy into a compatible one and use it'. This is essentially an ego-flawed assumption that a large number of people make and shows a distinct lack of experiential knowledge of the energy reality we live in. You can only transform similar energy types — and only those which are below or at your level of vibration. Anything at a higher level will change you and anything too different will disrupt your entire energy system. In effect, you are weakening your Self or becoming something which is not-Self.

The main exception to this is the principle which states that you can change the lower vibrations which are similar to your own. In the days of old, this was applied by Seidr practitioners where they would take Thrall energy which vibrated to a much lower frequency than that of the Jarls and fuel themselves with it. Some practice it with the Karls, too, due to the same principles being at play but they were far more selective since it required greater effort to absorb. We also find this playing a very prominent role in Seidr sexual mysteries, which will be covered at a later time. What we need to do to reclaim our energy and those micro-fragments of ourselves is some work with the Minni and Hugr which hold the access points.

The process is inherently simple but tedious to do. However, it is worth every second of time invested. This will not only reclaim what you have left behind or has been taken from you but will also unravel those bindings you have within daily life, as well as free you of the constant influences which drag you to the past.

Start by sitting with back straight, your feet touching (and making contact with the floor), your hands on the thighs and relax. In the following instructions, if you have mastered unleashing intent, then do it. If not, just think intensely of the energy body.

Chant the ᛒ Bjarkan (Berkano) rune and feel the Minni in its green glow rising from within you and landing in the form of a bird on your left shoulder. Typically, most visualise it as a raven in synchronicity with Oðin's ravens. Will it to guide you to the memories you need. Then do the same with the ↑ Týr (Tiwaz) rune and see the Hugr Raven rise in its blue glow in the same type of bird form as the Minni but landing your right shoulder. Will it to enable your perceptions of the recalled events to be clear and sharp.

This completes the preparation. If you struggle with the visualisations of the Minni and Hugr, do not worry about it. The intent will drive them forth. Even if they are not clearly felt, it is not an issue since they will be active nonetheless. It is just a lack of perception on your part, not a lack of presence on their part.

Whilst sitting with back straight, drop your chin to the right shoulder and move it to the left as far as you can go, making a half circle motion from right to left. As you do so you will be exhaling while chanting the ᚠ Óss (Ansuz) rune. Then move the chin from left to right and inhale whilst doing so, chanting the ◇ Ing (Ingwaz) rune if a biological male, ᛒ Bjarkan (Berkano) if a biological female. Do this a few times until it flows nicely. Once again for clarification:

1. Right to Left -> Exhale and chant ᚠ Óss (Ansuz)
2. Left to Right -> Inhale and chant ◇ Ing (Ingwaz) if you are a biological male or ᛒ Bjarkan (Berkano) if you are a biological female DO NOT mix these up. We will discuss these permutations of masculinity and femininity in their respective publications.

One you have settled into the flow of this, think back on an event or person you know. Recall as many details about them as you can, such as the places you interacted in, your emotional state whilst interacting with them, how they were responding, etc. Go into as much detail as possible. Do this AND keep the runic chanting and movement of the head going at the SAME time. What takes place is actually very simple, the ᚠ Óss (Ansuz) rune combined with exhale will throw out any alien (non-Self) energy. The inhale and ◇ Ing (Ingwaz) or ᛒ Bjarkan (Berkano) runes will pull back any of your misplaced energy.

When you are done with your recall or want to stop the practice for the time being, simply will the Hugr and Minni to return to their home positions in the brain and observe them remerge into it.

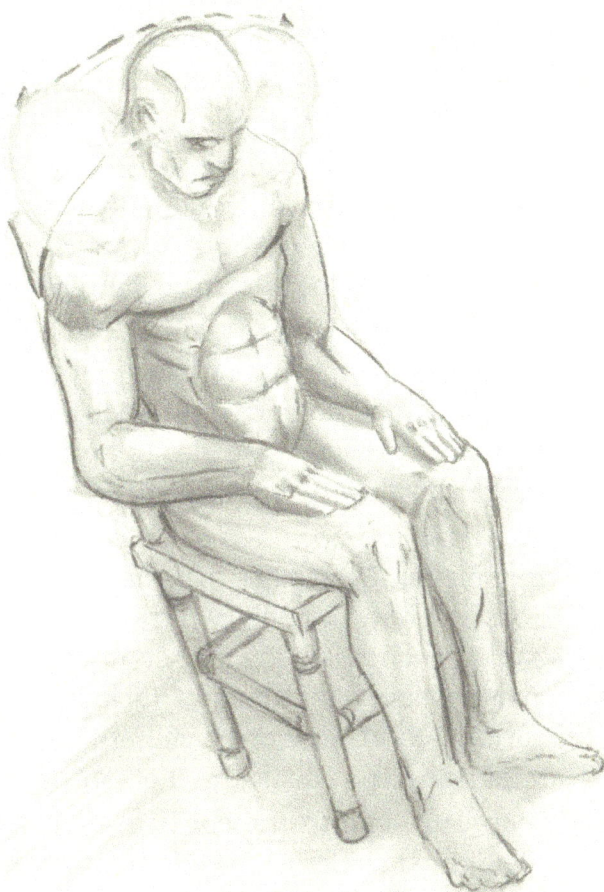

Energy Reclaiming Practice
Head down doing semi-clockwise motion

Quick Steps

1. Sit in a position with straight back and feet touching the ground, hands on your thighs and relax. Think of the memories of a given person or event or life experience.

If you have mastered intent, use it to unleash the respective memory.

2. Chant the rune ᛒ Bjarkan (Berkano) and feel the Minni in its green glow rising from within you landing on your left shoulder.

3. Will the Minni Raven to guide you to the memories you need. You will work with the first one which 'pops' into your awareness.

4. Do the same with the rune ᛏ Týr (Tiwaz) and see the Hugr Raven rising in its bluish glow and land on your right shoulder. Will it to cause all your memories to be detailed, sharp and clear when recalled.

5. Recall each memory in as much detail as you can muster. Remember the smallest details possible, how you felt, what you thought, and experienced during that event or in that memory about that person. Include all the actions. In other words, you are not only recalling a picture but a full set of experiences.

6. Drop your chin to the chest move it from the right shoulder to the left shoulder with chin against right shoulder, chest, left shoulder forming a semi circle, then reverse things so you move from left back to chest and right. Repeat this cycle as you recall each memory. Whilst going from right to left, exhale and chant ᚠ Óss (Ansuz) while willing the energy from the people or that event to be thrown out of you. When going from left to right, inhale and chant ◇ Ing (Ingwaz) (if biological male) or ᛒ Bjarkan (Berkano) (if biological female) whilst willing the

energies you left in with that person or in that event back into yourself.

7. When done, simply will the Hugr and Minni to fly back into their respective brain regions.

Here, you are achieving a reclaiming of your Self through your energy. Each person and experience you have ever encountered needs to be gone through. It is a long process but essential. Pulling back what is yours and throwing out what is not will free you up. This will also unbind you from traumatic events in life that impact your energy body (Hamr). People who have energetic links into you and are constantly pulling on your energy will be disconnected. In this manner, we disconnect from the past, release it and, most importantly, release ourselves from it. We disconnect from those who drain our attention and energy and pull back what is ours which they have taken and are dragging through goodness knows what. We also disconnect our Ørlog from theirs and unweave our Wyrd from theirs. Yes, once you share energies, you share fates. Ever heard of someone dragging you down and making a nightmare of your life? Well, this is how it happens in the bigger picture. Always be extremely careful with whom you share energy and connect. Someone who is highly positive and very evolved spiritually will uplift you to heights you cannot even imagine but someone whose life is filled with problems, unrealistic goals and loaded with what we term 'baggage' will drag you down with them. You can resist it at first but as more and more of you is pulled down, you will eventually fall or burn out trying to counter it. Set your energy free and you will be able to fly!

The other vital part of this practice is with technology. Here, the resulting exchange can only be termed
extremely damaging. The issue of how it impacts our
health has already been covered in 'The Spirit of
Húnir Awakens (Part 1)'[7]. What is relevant here is
the energetic exchange. Technology does not generate
living energy at all. What it does generate is a sticky
fluid-like energy which drains and locks down energy,
making it static. It is similar to sugar caramelising.
Technological energy does exactly that to biological
energy, changing free flowing energy into something
which appears thicker and stickier with electric currents.
It appears dark because it absorbs whatever it touches
and hence does not reflect or produce light of any
type. It shares a lot of the characteristics of nothingness and one can think of it as leading to nothingness,
just as Helheim is the first step to Niflheim which
leads to the Ginnungagap but in an artificially imposed
manner.

This non-living energy always affects us in a
negative fashion. The reason for this is simply due
to the fact that all non-living things absorb and
consume living energy in order to stay alive. The only
place from where it can get this life energy is from
living bio-organisms. When we watch movies on the
television, play online games, or watch things which
generate a strong emotional pulse, we experience the
same type of energy exchange that we do with others
in life. The emotions and exchanges are the same for
us irrespective of whether we are interacting with
a living or non-living 'thing'. However, since what we
are interacting with is an artificial (non-living) thing,
we are getting back a change in our energy rather

than a new energy. As mentioned above, this causes the effect of our own energy going sluggish and static. Even when using it to interact with others, we get some of their energy tainted with this technological (sticky stasis inducing) energy. This results from that person's energy which has been partially consumed by the technological energy combined with that very 'staining' sticky-stasis as it has absorbed on its way to you. In effect, we exchange a greater part of us for an even lesser part of them with the added 'bonus' of this energy, which is corruptive to our systems. With the advent of pure animations, virtual reality and robotic interactions, we get a complete total zero living energy for an exchange of our life giving energy. This is because we are not interacting with a living being but purely digital non-living creations. It is now in a position to literally feed on our Selves and give nothingness in return. A most dangerous state of affairs indeed! As it grows, we diminish and as it becomes more 'intelligent', we lose ours.

Naturally, as we become more aware and our perceptual abilities grow, we simply are no longer able to accept this form of loss of Self. So practicing this reclaiming and expulsion in the context of technological exchange is even more important to the modern-day mystic than it could ever have been previously. Instead of focussing on memories in terms of people we know, here we focus on interactions with cyberspace and technology. The impact is often felt immediately and the differences felt extremely sharply. This is even more true for the younger generation which has become totally addicted and dependant on this artificial energy exchange. You cannot free your mind if you enslave it to technology. Throw its energy out of your Self and you will be able to observe a dramatic change in both the Minni and Hugr activity and, if you pay close attention, you will see subtle yet profound changes in conscious awareness. Regardless, whether you consciously notice changes or not, this energetic reclaiming will greatly amplify the results of all work involving the Óðr, Minni and Hugr, as well as those related to conscious awareness and perception.

AN IMPORTANT NOTE FOR MEN

This technological energy, as well as all other artificially produced energies, is very feminine. Just as the chemical changes to our environment are highly estrogenic, so is this. Chemicals, technology and artificial changes to natural things are all producing an unnatural feminine energy. It is causing a whole range of issues with women but it is even more destructive for men. It is simply because men are evolving away from the feminine and instead of enabling them to do so, this artificial feminine energy is 'gluing them' back into the feminine from which they are evolving. This is so destructive that it is giving rise to what we see as the effeminate male in the modern era or the ergi male as the Norse used to term it. In the past, it was just a matter of loss of masculinity due to an overload of feminine energy (all energy in Creation is predominantly feminine, and masculine energy is extremely rare). In the modern world, however, we have all this artificial energy to worry about which is not only feminine in nature but is overwhelmingly so. To put it in context, artificially estrogenic substances bind to biological receptors 100,000s times longer and exert stronger activation than their natural counterparts.

Doing this reclaiming with cyberspace interactions and technology is EVEN more important than doing it with natural events and personal interactions if you are a man. Men should all start with these first and foremost and then progress to interactions with people and life events. Women, on the other hand, should stick to the opposite. For men, this can wield a surprising reassurance of masculinity and self-confidence as well as be very empowering energetically as the masculine current is explosive and life creating.

BREAKING THE SHACKLES
OF THE MIND

REMOVING LIMITATIONS
OF THE MIND

You might remember that we looked at most of the limitations of the mind in Part 1 of 'The Spirit of Húnir Awakens'. Most the work in Part 1 involved becoming aware of the limitations imposed upon us by social conditioning, relying on language, thinking and over-thinking in certain ways, complying with set belief systems and self-limiting ourselves via self perceptions as well as the impact of technology, desires, passivity of will, collectivism and scientific reliance. Awareness of them and how they impact us was the first step in freeing ourselves from their grasp. As you will have noticed, the work in Part 2 makes great strides in the removal of those limitations, strengthening mental perceptive skills and abilities in order to avoid falling back into these limitations. By freeing ourselves of those initial limitations and undertaking the work here in Part 2, you will achieve the unshackling of our minds which enables us to step beyond the reach of them all.

LIMITATIONS OF EMOTION

The final important limitation to be removed is that of emotion. We have looked at the energetic damage that emotional outbursts and intense emotional experiences can create in 'The Breath of Odin Awakens'[8], and they will be discussed in greater detail when looking at the energy body (Hamr). For the time being, it is important to understand that emotions not only serve to deprive us of the energy used to fuel them and attract more of the same on the mental level but they also bind us. Love and hate are the two greatest offenders in this context but we will look at them at a later time. Suffice it to say that emotion is a physiological and chemical response to what we experience in our environments (be that mental or physical or even energetic). Our culture and socialisation has made us all too obsessed with emotions to the point of addiction. It is time to abandon dreamlike-vague concepts and embrace matters in terms of practical approaches that lead to action, rather than drowning in emotional cycles and worrying about feeling this or that. All these are pure entrapment for the mind, perception and awareness. It is time to cut through all of that and strike at our actual purpose: realisation of the Self and survival as individuals.

REMOVING FUNDAMENTAL MISUNDERSTANDINGS OF THE FLESH

This one is very important. All too often in various belief systems, philosophies and so-called awakening systems, there are concepts that purport that the body (Lik) is unimportant, something to be overcome and rejected. Others include individuals who actually hate their bodies, reject them, or seem to wilfully harm them. All such behaviours and beliefs serve only to cause turmoil in one of the core parts of the Self (the body – Lik). As we will see in the next work, the physical body (Lik) is not only essential for our spiritual evolution and development of awareness but it is also an extremely opportunity to complete our work at unifying the entire Self into a whole. Without the body (Lik), no such work is possible and hence no wisdom or power is accessible. The other problem that being in disharmony or conflict with the body (Lik) creates is that as soon as it dies or something catastrophic happens to it, then it is the end for us if we have not completed our unified Self. There is no such thing as reincarnation of the personality. Those nonsensical belief systems are designed to induce a disregard for the physical body (Lik), often thinking along the lines of 'I do not like it here, so I'll come back and try again somewhere or some time else'.

This is one of the biggest delusions of our time. When the body dies, the energy body (Hamr) separates and starts a gradual dissolution process (because the physical body (Lik) gave it cohesion and energy). The Minni gets absorbed by the Fylgja, the spirit (Óðr) constricts inwards until it simply turns into a single point and then the Önd stops flowing. The Fylgja returns to the ancestral stream with a summary of all the experiences gained and the memories of the Minni, while the mind-reason (Hugr) is either gifted or stays bound to the shadow (Sal) where, combined, they either haunt somewhere, go to Helheim or another resting place. The Hamingja returns to the ancestral stream and fuses with the totality of ancestral Megin (unless gifted). The Self itself is torn apart. The remaining parts carry something of you but are not you. This is why we strive so hard to attain unification of the Self and for that we NEED the physical body (Lik) in as good a shape or state of being as possible. We will look more closely at the entire death process in due course as well as at the various options one has when it comes to circumventing the default split and loss of the Self.

REMOVING LIMITATIONS OF TIME

Our modern life has imposed a very interesting yet totally crippling binding on our minds and spirits, namely Time. Practically every second of our lives is pinned down to a time. We get up at a certain time, we have breakfast at a certain time and leave for work by a certain time. Each and every day is centred around these specific points in time. Additionally, being surrounded by watches and other time telling devices has our minds constantly locked down and stress-driven all just to comply with time. This is not as innocent as you think! Repetition locks the mind, restricts perception and binds awareness to the here and now. We will discuss the exact nature of time elsewhere (which incidentally is NOT linear as we are conditioned to see it). For now, you will need to loosen those shackles of human imposed time. Stop wearing a watch, keep time keeping devices OUT of your bedroom, ignore them on your pc, simply each time time comes up just think 'I don't care' or 'it's irrelevant', then shift your focus onto whatever else you can do. This will be tricky but once the habituation of time is abandoned, life becomes less stressful and you allow the flow of time to alter for you. When entering other modes of awareness, you will be able to gain years, if not decades, worth of experiences and yet only invest a few hours or just minutes of human-counted time.

This does not mean that you should never refer to time, however! Unfortunately, living here in Midgard, you will have little choice but to obey the clock at times but the more detached you become from its cycle when you can, the less impact it will have on your spirit (Óðr).

INTENT

The Great Mystery of Intent

Intent is a very important concept to grasp and is an extremely important skill to master. It is what fuels action, movement, motion and evolution itself. On the energetic side of reality, all is based around intent. It is the foundation of everything else you will ever do, in one way or another. Without it, nothing happens. Actually the more you move from the physical into the deeper layers of energetic existence, you will get to the point where nothing can exist without intent. It is a simple principle of 'no intent – no existence' because at those levels, intent is what causes existence. It is, in fact, existence's fundamental cause.

What exactly is intent?

There is no point in discussing the dictionary definition of intent because here we are focussing on the fundamental action of Spirit (Óðr) and not of its tool (the mind). Linguistics are capped at the mind level. We are seeking to move beyond the ceiling of the intellect, which is most difficult to convey in writing. We will try and formulate as much of it as possible to guide you to the actuality of intent. You will have to use the following information as a map towards the nature and experience of intent, not as a 'this is it' type of indicator. Why so? Intent is felt, or to be more precise, it is sensed and experienced. It is not thought or reasoned. Remember the sense of the Spirit (Óðr)? That is how you know intent as a direct sensory input at the level of your spirit (Óðr).

Let us hence try to conceptualise intent. Broadly speaking, it can be thought of as an impulse of the Will manifesting from within your own spirit into the outer or inner worlds. In other words, it is a manifest-ation of the most subtle form of activity of the Spirit (Óðr), the Spark of Self sending out an impulse of what it wills. This gives intent a cohesive energetic manifestation. Intent has energy, direction, flow and purpose. It expresses the Will of the Spirit (Óðr) as well as its nature. Understanding what our Will actually is, is also critical to gaining a solid concept of intent.

LIMITATIONS IMPOSED UPON INTENT

At this point in evolution, intent is limited in one key manner. It could only manifest at the mental level of reality. Without a physical body (Lik), it was unable to intend at the energetic and physical levels of existence. When discussing the energy level, it is important to keep in mind that what is being described is not that the mental level lacks energy — quite the contrary. It is a totally flurry of energetic flows but there is no cohesive energy substance. It is a level of thought which directs energy rather than a level of energy per se. Only once the cohesion of energy takes place and forms energetic substance, which in turn becomes cohesive in its own right, that we get an energetic level of existence. This is another one of those highly abstract concepts but it will make sense as you awaken various parts of the Self. They will help you understand these abstractions with such ease that you will at that point wonder what the fuss what all about. Once the Spirit (Óðr) has gained manifestation into a physical form and formed its energetic form, it becomes capable of expressing intent in its completeness. This is one of the primary reasons why we learn to express intent on the mental level first and then progress onto the energetic. We are in effect following the flow of manifestation and enhancing the totality of possible ways for intent to be expressed.

At that point, intent is still the expression of the Will of Óðr as an impulse streaming from it, but it also gains a distinct energetic quality to it AND gains the expression of conscious awareness. It no longer is one but is now three principles flowing in union. This is true complete intent. As such, in order to learn how to intend, the learning has to be done at both the mental level via the practices of the spirit (Óðr) and at the physical level via the practices of the energy body (Hamr). Only then can we unleash true intent. It is this form of intent which shapes realities and the Self, which is why when using High Galdr, understanding and developing one's ability to practically use intent is so vitally important. It is one of its fundamentals which turns Galdr from just repetitive chanting of the runic names into actual expression of reality shaping intent (High Galdr). This is why Húnir's gift is so important to us all, as it is the perfect way to express higher forms of consciousness in Midgard.

The methods for mastering intent span across many practices in this work. Let us then move onto the first part of these without further ado.

It is of vital importance to master intent. The full capabilities of it once all the parts are combined is a direct manifestation of one's actual Spark of Self. Fuelled by the power of Megin-filled breath (Önd), rooted in the energy body (Hamr) and flowing through the spirit (Óðr), intent is the root of all power. Ensure you master this and all parts of the intent well. It is an essential key. Work on your intent, strengthen it, empower it each and every day. Unleash it over and over again. Unleash multiple intents simultaneously. Keep pushing forth more and more. Develop and enhance your intent every moment you can. All future work will require intent mastery.

Pure Thought – Key to the Óðr Intent (Stage 1)

We have said much with respect to the mind-reason (Hugr) thus far but little practical groundwork with respect to the spirit (Óðr) has been presented. it is time for that to change! Communicating with the spirit (Óðr) is a little tricky, to say the least, but once you get used to it, it becomes the easiest thing you can do. Because the spirit (Óðr) is the thought processor and generator, you cannot com-municate in terms of linguistic thought. As soon as you add words to your thoughts, they are no longer abstract enough to reach the spirit (Óðr) and instead reach the Hugr-Minni level. This is why so many people struggle with even becoming aware of their spirit (Óðr). What we need to use in order to communicate is what can be termed pure thought.

The best way to comprehend pure thought is to think of it in terms of meaning or conceptions of what you want to communicate rather than the words you would use to label it. For instance, if you try to tell it to expand your awareness, you would focus on sensing what the meaning behind expansion of awareness is. It is extremely difficult to explain but it is a type of sensing what the words are trying to describe. This sense flows either directly to where you are aiming your communication or through the energies you send out and receive. You are basically wrapping thousands of words into a single sense of meaning. This will take time to master but once things click and you understand what you are trying to do, it will become child's play. In order to do this from a practical perspective, all you need to do is to learn how to convey what you would in terms of words but without ever using a word, and then imagine feeling what you are trying to convey. It is a subtle type of sensing of meaning wrapped in non-verbal thought. The best way to try and explain it is simply to try to perceive how you decide to cross a street, or do something physically in the automated way you do without thinking about it. For instance, when you walk you are moving but you do not think about the moving. We have no need to think 'ok I'm going forward for 10 paces then moving a little to the left or right and then turning around'. Instead, we just intend to do this without forming a single actual set of thoughts using words. We move using intent wrapped in pure thought. The same happens when you pick up a cup and make tea. It is automatic yet also directed, thoughtlessly.

Once you master pure thought, you have in effect mastered the mental part of actual intent. When working with energy, be it runic energy or energy of any other type, intent plays an essential role. Typically, one would attempt to manipulate and direct energy with thought alone; however herein lies a big problem. How the energy you work with interprets the directing thought(s) will depend on the energy and whether you can think abstractly enough to filter out the human thinking patterns and idiosyncrasies. Using intent rather than just thought avoids the entire problem, allowing you to intend a desired result in such an abstract manner that any type of energy will natively understand what you want it to do. This removes the entire problem of things not manifesting or manifesting in not quite the way you want them to, all of which are results of 'interpretation' of thoughts. Remember you are in effect communicating with the underlying consciousness or rather awareness of that energy.

For instance, if you send out some healing via the ᚾ Úr (Uruz) rune to your partner and think heal him/her, typically you would visualise that limb (such as a leg) which is injured. The runic energy will be confused as to whether it is healing the physical leg, what part of it, when, how or is it healing the energetic counterpart of the leg? Is it both? Does it heal from physical to energetic? Or the other way round? What do you mean by healing? If you try to pack all that information in, you risk even more misinterpretations when using words. Then you have the issue of energy specific interpretations and adaptations. Healing in terms of ᚾ Úr (Uruz) is regeneration. It would not be very effective for a flu. However, if you think 'heal' in context of ᚦ Þurs (Thurisaz), that would work on the flu as it would attack and strike at the actual virus. If you think 'heal' for regeneration in terms of

89

ᚦ Þurs (Thurisaz), it will cause tissue breakdown and inflammation in order to initiate the body's own repair mechanism rather than actually heal. As you can see, this subtle difference of adaptation of the term 'heal' causes a lot of problems.

With pure thought, the meaning behind the term heal is used instead, programming each energy automatically. So if you use the pure thought of 'heal' and ᚦ Þurs (Thurisaz), aiming it at the torn muscle, it will not cause tissue breakdown but rather quicken blood flow and increase neural conductivity there which helps the body rebuild or heal faster. This is a very important difference.

Do not let this complexity bog you down for the time being. Simply work at learning pure thought until you have mastered it.

Mental Protection

Many will wonder why there has been no discussion of protection at the mental level of reality or with respect to the mental level of the Self. The underlying reason for this is that there is no actual need of it. Initially, this might seem a very odd statement in view of all the previous emphasis on protection. The reason for this has to do with how this level of reality operates. Do you recall from the discussions on thoughts and energy and from Part 1 of 'The Spirit of Húnir Awakens' that whatever you think, you automatically 'connect' with? This in itself is the key to understanding why protection is unnecessary. Simply refusing to think about something harmful to you will block it out. By excluding the offending or harmful thoughts from our mental Self, we are automatically preventing them from manifesting on the energetic, thus short-circuiting their manifestation in our daily lives. In this way, we are also automatically preventing ourselves from powering them and turning our own minds into our greatest enemy. It is for this reason that we put so much effort into mastering our thoughts and controlling our thinking.

Incidentally, this is also the basis on which all of those modern-day practices that state if you reject this or that, you then deny it in your life. People incorrectly assume that it will limit the rejected events, people or energy from reaching them physically and smooth out their lives. This type of work only affects the mental if something is already manifesting on the energetic level of reality. In that case, you do indeed need the appropriate protections in place as it has already begun to manifest. If, however, they are only forming on the mental, then it will work.

Having said all this, there is a possibly of being targeted by thought forms on the mental level of reality. That is unavoidable and needs to be dealt with. In order to do so, simply practice the stillness of the mind skills you have already developed and intend any obsessive thoughts to leave without ever being able to return. This type of rejection fuelled by a stilled mind is powerful beyond anything you might imagine. They will strike with such precision and overwhelming force that whatever is trying to enter your mental Self will instantly shatter.

THE MINNI

THE MINNI – KEY TO MEMORY

Memories are references to specific point in time and space. The Minni creates, writes, retrieves and stores personal memories and enlivens them. Once it accesses the relevant reference, it will connect conscious awareness through the Hugr to the referenced event. When recalled from the spirit (Óðr), we transfer their essence into it. In effect, this creates a link or thread from the reference point to the actual event on both the mental and spiritual levels.

It can only store these reference points and links to the actual memories for a 'brief' time. This would be the equivalent of short-term memory which, with a little training, could be pushed to medium-term memory. The place where it actually writes these millions upon billions of reference points is the energy body (Hamr). Upon death, rather than allowing all these to be lost when it dissolves (assuming of course that you have not yet attained eternity of the energy body (Hamr)), the Fylgja sets to work (assuming you have still not realised your Self fully). It siphons all these reference points by temporarily fusing with the Minni.

When the Minni and Fylgja merge in this way, the Minni's ability to look all these memories up goes into overdrive. It will go through the countless linking threads to all the memories you have ever had (even those you are unable to recall). For each of them, the actual energetic imprint of each event is extracted into its essence and absorbed by the Fylgja. Once every memory and experience have been funnelled into the Fylgja, it separates from the rest of the Self in a massive energetic outburst and re-joins the ancestral lines. Ultimately, it seeks out the memories of all those life experiences which are considered key and all those which make you what you are, who you are and what lead you to your becoming that person. This merging is really what people who are near death experience when they say they saw 'their lives flash before their eyes'. It is a side-effect of the accessing and gathering of memory essence by the Fylgja via the Minni. Once it has gathered the memories linking to those life experiences, it will then collect all the associated life essence and store it within the ancestral pools of power.

Understanding time and how it inter-relates to Ørlǫg is important in order to gain a solid under-standing on how memory actually works. Unfortunately, it is a topic which will have to be covered in greater detail at a later point in time. For the time being, a few pointers will have to suffice.

Time is not linear. It is only perceived as being linear due to the way in which our brains function and the social conditioning we have all been subjected to since our childhoods. The counting of time in terms of hours, minutes and seconds is an artificial imposition of a concept of time on our minds. This is then reinforced on a constant basis. We are surrounded by computers, watches and time measuring devices practically on a constant basis. Unfortunately, time does not function in the manner in which we are accustomed to understanding it. It is not linear. In other words, when looked at from a higher level of reality it flows in a non-constant, non-linear fashion. It can flow forwards, backwards and even skip through entire ages and periods. It can flow in a circular fashion, criss-cross other time flows and so on. It is important to keep in mind that not everything flows in one-time stream/flow but in an infinite number of them. We will delve into much more detail on time and its influences in a future publication whilst looking at Ørlǫg and the Norns. For the time being, keep in mind that you are not dealing with a linear flow. Hence a future event can occur in the past even though you are in the present and have not experienced that event yet yourself.

Memories are extremely powerful tools for our awareness. They are formed in the past and only the past. When people speak of things such as future memories, they mistakenly attribute a past perception of a future event and label it as a future memory. From the current human perspective, it is a memory of a future event but it was perceived in the past hence the rule of memories being reference points to past events hold correct. Once awareness has progressed to the point where time and space are correctly perceived as fluid state (which let us keep in mind scientists are well aware of and have been for a long time) then a more accurate understanding takes hold. This understanding allows us to not only work with memories per se when working with the Minni and the Fylgja but also with the actual powers they hold. This power pointed to by the memory (which is a key for accessing them) are referred to as the essence of the memories.

Why are memories so important? They provide us with links back in time and back to the events which lead to their formation. Just as there are an unlimited number of levels of awareness, so too there are unlimited sources of experiences and events, and hence also memory sources. The human mind only taps into the most minute of these. Even labelling that range as a 1% would be a gross overstatement. It is more akin to 0.00000000001%. Nonetheless, what is experienced is immensely useful.

Since memories are a record of experience, they hold energy, a state of being, a state of mind, a perception, an energetic pattern of the Self, a cohesion of the world at the time of the experience and a connection to all the things which existed at that point in time and space. Why should this matter to us? Simply because that is an extremely potent key to both runic energy manipulation and manipulation of perceptual capabilities!

MEMORIES AND THE HUMAN BRAIN
NEURAL BASIS OF REMEMBERING

When looking at memory with respect to the physical body (Lik), we naturally need to focus on the brain. However, before we do so, it is worth remembering that we have a nervous system which extends throughout the entire body comprised of millions upon millions of cells with micro-consciousnesses of their own. When you look at memory, you need to keep in mind that all those parts of your physicality just like your energy body (Hamr) will be remembering and learning in their own respect. They, too, have memory which works through changes in their states of being or function. For instance, memory is expressed biologically as structures of neurons, how they connected to each other, what electrical impulses they give off, in which pattern, how they communicate chemically and electrically with each other and so forth. Upon learning, things change and the inter-connectedness, structures and functions shift. A similar process takes place on the cellular level too. This is biological memory which functions irrespective of our conscious awareness and, in a lot of instances, even irrespective of the spirit (Óðr) itself. Take note of this, because it leads to an important insight: that memory can mean very different things based on what part of your Self you are referring to.

Let us move back into the more traditional view of memory, the remembrance of events and things with which our minds work. For practically everyone, those are brain dependant. Naturally, scientists have an utter obsession with memory and learning and are desperate to understand it in order to manipulate it. Unfortunately for the sciences, they have made as little progress over the years as would be typically expected — in other words, they still have no firm idea or concept of how it all actually works. Initially, we had the 'established' understanding that a tiny part of the brain called the hippocampus was responsible for memory. This then changed to being responsible only for certain types of memories. Eventually it moved onto the fact that it shared memory function with countless other parts of the brain, such as the amygdala for emotion and fear based memories, the frontal cortex for short term memory and so forth. Now we are at the stage where concepts of brain-wide memory storage are being considered.

The Centre for Consciousness Studies at the University of Arizona published their findings in 2012 on how memory was not based on the connections or activations of neurons or rather how those were short lived but is instead embedded at a molecular level[9]. In effect, the entire understanding of memory is changing. They still are struggling to understand that the structural (neural) adaptations are related to purely biological memory (how the brain manages its references) but there is progress in terms of looking deeper. As we will see when dealing with the energy level of our Self it is at the molecular level that energy hits and activates a projection of memory back into the Hugr (and hence conscious awareness/perception).

When looking at memory on the physical, it is a well-known fact that women are better at remembering and have an uncanny ability to retain detail. We have seen in 'The Spirit of Húnir Awakens (Part 1)'[10] how the wiring of the male and female brains differs and this contributes to the ladies' strengths in terms of memory. When looking at this phenomenon, we need to keep in mind that the energetic parts of the Self that deal with memory are female in nature. It is this condensing characteristic of the feminine current which enables memories to 'stick' and be transmitted without loss of energy. Because the Minni and Fylgja are both feminine in nature, this gives all the ladies out there a massive advantage over the gents.

The gents have an upper-hand elsewhere, however, as memory on the energetic level of the Self is highly active and therefore the energy body (Hamr) deals with memories and remembering without having to recourse to the Minni at all. When we access them in our standard mode of consciousness, the Minni works to bridge them to us but otherwise the energy body (Hamr) itself does the remembering, very much like the bio-logical memory of our physical bodies.

Why all this confusion? Simply because even for modern day science, there is an inability to grasp the underlying concept that what they think of as memories are nothing more than references or pointers to memories. What the brain stores is a type of 'this is where I will find this bit of information and I need to go look for it there' for each memory. Those memories are then stored in the energetic and mental levels of reality. Ah, but the brain is just physical and cannot access those you think... Yes and no. The brain is physical but it can access non-physical realities because the physical is nothing more or less than very dense energy and is therefore part of the energetic levels of reality. Want proof? In a study looking at the structures and functions of neurons, they found that the brain is multi-dimensional[11]. Not only that but when they used mathematics in combination with neurosciences, they discovered that it can function, in some cases, in up to all 11 dimensions![12] Thus science has just embarked on the path of validating all of our ancestral knowledge. It is just a start but a good one. In the advanced work we will look at later on, we will see how the Seidr practitioners and Æsir have practices that can extend and amplify the reach of our brains (and hence physicality) into those additional dimensions. For now, however, let us stick to the task at hand.

MEMORIES AND THE
ENERGY BODY (HAMR)

Even though we are not really going to focus much on the Self at the energetic level of reality right here, it is worth doing so briefly in order to look at how memory functions in the energy body (Hamr) and just touch upon its function in the shadow body (Sal).

We are primarily energy, both subtle (Hamr level with no mass) and dense (physical Lik level with mass). We have just had a look at how the physical body (Lik) deals with memories by building neural structures in the brain and other relevant parts of our physiology. Those are primarily memories which pertain to our physical lives and experiences gained by way of the body (Lik). The same applies to the energy body (Hamr), but due to the lack of matter, it builds those memories into the energy itself. These points are primarily built into what is referred to as the auric field. It is interesting to note that our Fylgja resides in this auric field as well. The boundaries of the auric field or the surface of the human energy bubble (both inner and outer) are the only permanent parts of the energy body. They do not flow and they are kept intact by the cohesive power of our awareness. It could also be said that the cohesive power of the energy field enables our awareness to be. This cohesive force arises out of the ᛇ Jór (Eihwaz) rune's influence as it interacts with our Spark of Self. For those who have fully awoken their Spark of Self, this underlying force undergoes a subtle yet significant change. During this change, the cohesive effect now becomes a direct result of the interactions of ᛇ Jór (Eihwaz) and the archetypal manifestation of the ᛋ Sól (Sowilo) rune. When the Spark eventually shifts into a Divine Spark, the triangulation of the Self is complete and the interaction then becomes centred in the action of ᛋ Sól (Sowilo), ᛇ Jór (Eihwaz) and ᛦ Ýr (Elhaz). That, however, is very advanced work so we will stick to the basics for the time being.

Within the energy body (Hamr), perception flows very differently from what we are typically used to in our daily lives. Everything flows in filaments (or lines if you prefer). For memory to 'stick', it needs a slightly more solid place to be recorded or it will simply flow onwards and away. This is where the auric field or energy bubble of the human being comes into play. When we look at the energy body (Hamr) in more detail, we will see how this can and has to change for us to evolve onwards but for now, it is what it is. The function of the Minni is to act as a mechanism where memories from non-physical experiences are stored on the inner surface (mostly) and sometimes the outer surface of this bubble shape. The actions of the Minni are a must whilst we work on maturing the energy body (Hamr) until it can act as a proper vehicle for conscious awareness. This is what virtually our entire life's work is all about. Because there is no direct link in between the mental level of the Self and the energy body (Hamr) per se, the Minni is the only intermediary for accessing, recording, and manipulating those memories of events and knowledge that we gain whilst in higher (non-physical) modes of awareness. It is also the reason why things that happen in those states of awareness are very rapidly forgotten once we return to our usual modus operandi. Keep track of how easy or difficult it is for you to carry over the memories from those states of awareness back to normal daily thinking. The easier it becomes and the more detail you carry over, the stronger and more developed your Minni. The more unstable, unreliable and difficult the flow of information in between one state of mind and the other, the weaker the Minni or the less developed your awareness. As its ability to shift from one state to another is increased, eventually it will stretch to encompass those two states of mind on a constant basis.

REALITY LEVELS AND MEMORIES

Although we briefly touch on this above, let us expand a bit further into this topic. In order to remember across these shifts in states of awareness, we can engage with the Minni to perform a special type of linking. It is a rather abstract mechanism which is probably best explained by way of metaphor or it will become overwhelming very rapidly. To put it in computer-speak, you can think of awareness acting at each level of reality as being in a different state and spawning a separate yet inter-connected instance of itself. So you would have an instance of awareness functioning at the trance level and you would have a suspended instance of awareness back at the physical level. What typically happens is you deactivate the one used in trance and reactivate the one at the physical level. Because the awareness at the physical level did not experience the occurrences at the trance level, it has no memory of it and vice versa. Now the Minni inscribes those memories in the mental level of the Self. Because of the natural link of the Spirit

(Óðr) with the physical body (Lik), the two instances of your awareness are linked. The more you switch in-between them, the more you will remember. If you run through all the trance events immediately upon return to your physical awareness, you will transfer most, if not all, the memories to your physical awareness. Eventually, you will become so practiced that the physical instance of awareness and the trance instance both expand, causing them to overlap. With frequent overlap, they eventually merge and physical awareness expands and grows.

This is even trickier when using the energy body (Hamr) in dream walking, projections and energy work. Due to the lack of a natural physical linkage in between the two, we only have the action of the Minni here. You will have an instance of physical awareness in the background and functioning awareness in the energy body. The Minni will write all the experiences into the auric field. But since there is no linkage between the mental level awareness and the energy body awareness, memories cannot just pass in between the two. Instead, they pass in between the awareness of the physical body (Lik) and the energy body (Hamr) without the conscious awareness of the mental even being aware of them. Instead, you have a type of biological awareness and, as this expands closer and closer to the energy body, you will be totally oblivious to all of it as there is no mental action there. How to bridge these more effectively will be discussed once we look at the runes and cellular intelligence. But for now, you will mostly notice that you forget the experiences and learnings you have at the energy body (Hamr) activity when back in the physical body (Lik) but as soon as you shift back to the energy body (Hamr) you regain those memories with such perfect recall that you relive them. So take comfort that nothing is actually forgotten — it is just beyond your reach to remember until you develop the skills to do so. We will look at how to improve this situation later on.

ANCESTRAL MEMORIES & DNA
FYLGJA, KIN-FYLGJA
AND AETT-FYLGJA

When discussing genetic memories, most people have trouble grasping the concept of this possibility. The fact that we can transmit information, experiences, memories and even skill sets from generation to generation seems like the 'stuff' of science-fiction rather than fact to most. Well unfortunately for all, it is not only fact in terms of energetic realms but has now become fact in terms of scientific realms as well.

The scientific world has taken this most sacred part of our inheritance and life itself and is in the process of corrupting it to enable data storage. Oh yes, imagine you might soon be using your computers (or an alternate form of them) to write to your bloodstream. All those utterly useless terra bytes of information from social media could well be streaming, not only in your blood, but also in all your offspring's bloodstreams as well. And guess what? It might very well not only corrupt your inherited genetic data but could potentially make a mess of your entire DNA streams.

We are honestly a bit early for that in terms of technology but it is on its way. Scientists have been able to write, store and read data stored in DNA, the level of development is far ahead of what one would believe it to be as shown in this 2012 abstract:

> "Digital information is accumulating at an astounding rate, straining our ability to store and archive it. DNA is among the most dense and stable information media known. The development of new technologies in both DNA synthesis and sequencing make DNA an increasingly feasible digital storage medium. Here, we develop a strategy to encode arbitrary digital information in DNA, write a 5.27-megabit book using DNA microchips, and read the book using next-generation DNA sequencing."[13]

ExtremeTech Feb 2012 Edition Online goes deeper in this by looking at how machines made from biological molecules are being used to decode encrypted DNA. The author ends the article on a very concerning implication, stating, "Who's to say that, one day, we will not have a biotech implant that reads (or rewrites!) our DNA when needed? Imagine a future where you can store data in your bloodstream..."[14]

For those of you who are interested in this technology and its development, an excellent article is available in Nature magazine[15] which goes into good detail of potential and current applicability and scope. For our purposes, such in-depth study of the associated technology and sciences is not necessary because they are just re-inventing what we have already known for generations. The Eddas, Sagas and traditional accounts and teachings are filled with this knowledge, as well as how it is used and why. Science is just in the process of catching up! We will be looking at DNA, its functions and its runic uses in due course when studying the physical body (Lik) and the energy body (Hamr), where it plays a critically vital role. For now, suffice it to keep in mind that DNA has the capacity to store information. What they have yet to discover is that it stores so much more (hence one of the dangers when it comes to writing and rewriting DNA).

As for the question of whether memories are passed on, this has been subject to scientific enquiry as well. They have shown memories of fears triggered by specific odours passed from mother to offspring in animals where the lead researcher states:

"Our results allow us to appreciate how the experiences of a parent, before even conceiving offspring, markedly influence both structure and function in the nervous system of subsequent generations," Dr. Brian Dias of the Emory University department of psychiatry.[16]

Countless other studies have been published showing how primordial responses and fears are passed on from mother to child and that even though new-born human infants are not necessarily born with those fears, they acquire them exceptionally rapidly[17].

Such rapid acquisition of experiential knowledge is DNA based. A 2013 study published in Science looks at the mechanisms by which this is achieved on a genetic level, via the medium of what are called epigenetics (genes that turn other genes on or off)[18].

Leaving all this science to the side, let us look at what we are taught in the Norse tradition. It teaches us that certain parts of the Self are directly inherited through the ancestral lines such as the Fylgja, which forms an integral part of the archetypal level of the Self, linked into ancestral pools of knowledge, experience and power via the kin-Fylgja. At a 'higher' level we have the clan based inheritance of all these character-istics through the Ætt-Fylgja. Finally, at the peak of the familial carriers we have the embodiment of all these in the Disir. We will leave the more in-depth investigation of these living embodiments for the appropriate time and place. For now, they are discussed here to give us an understanding that certain things are inherited and this inheritance has a far greater impact on us all than we would have ever suspected.

Why bother with all of this? Essentially for a few key reasons. One is to understand that the modern day obsession with reincarnation is nothing more than a convenient illusion designed to promote individual stasis. Why worry about realisation of the Self in this lifetime when you could have so many more lives to continue your work? Unfortunately, this is not the case and all those failed Self realisations just provide fuel of one type or another, in energetic terms. The other reason we need to look into this is that by accessing these ancestral memories, knowledge, skills and abilities residing in our genetics, we can take advantage of all our ancestor's progress in terms of spiritual evolution right now. There is really no point in just worrying about contributing to that pool of experience just yet, so instead we are going to use all it has to offer to reach realisation and completion of ancestral lines. This is especially true for those who do not have children. First, we learn to access those which have been directly transmitted within our DNA, then later on we tap into those stored in the Fylgja, then the kin-Fylgja and finally the Ætt-Fylgja. Remember how we discussed thoughts giving rise to energy or pooling it? Just imagine what thought combined with experiential essence does. Yes, we are eventually going to be using as much of that as we possibly can.

Awakening ancestral memories requires accessing our DNA energetically. We will be covering this in great detail in the next work. For the time being, it is worth keeping in mind that these can awaken spontaneously as you work with the other memory systems of the Self in the practices in this section. If you absolutely want to target ancestral memories right now, use the Memory Ale practices given below but do be careful — once they start to stir, they can overwhelm you very easily.

MEMORY AND ENERGY

The relationship of energy and memory is so important it is impossible to understate it. Not only is it prevalent in terms of the non-physical types of memory that we have (and hence the non-Lik parts of the Self) but it is so even on the physical. Let us look into that before shifting to the less well known parts.

According to the laws of energy and memory, the former is needed to access and use the latter. It makes sense when you think about it — getting the memory, writing it, processing it, looking it up all those are activities which require some sort of fuel to carry out. The brain is highly electrical when it comes to energy use profiles. Electrical pulses are generated by the neurons from their activity fuelled by primarily glucose and ketones (from fats) as emergency fuels. Now, since memory requires energy to be accessed and used, what do you think happens when the amount of energy diminishes, either due to lack thereof or due to the brain systems not be able to process that energy it has available? Memory suffers, getting to the memories is harder and they take longer to access. When the energy runs very low, it slowly becomes less and less possible to even access those memories. Do note that we are not discussing forgetting. We are looking at the inability to get to the memories. This can be confused with forgetting since if you cannot get access to them, you in effect do not remember. But those memories are not 'forgotten' per se — they are still there. Actual forgetting implies that the memory is lost, gone or simply no longer in existence while this is just an issue of accessibility not loss of the memory.

When it comes to the physical brain, this effect is most prominent in the highly energy demanding parts of it. Incidentally, these are the parts where the Hugr and Minni 'house' themselves. In other words, the pre-frontal cortex, the part of the brain just behind your forehead where all the logic processing, reasoning and consciousness reside, along with a specific type of memory called 'working memory'. This is the part of the brain which uses enormous amounts of glucose (sugars) to fuel itself. The Minni is very active in that part of the brain, as well as the right side and the back of the brain (typically referred to as the 'small brain' or cerebellum in scientific circles). The Hugr on the other hand has primary activity on the front (frontal cortex) and left side of the brain. A recent study looked at the issue with energy availability in the brain and concluded that it was not the so called 'loss of neurons' due to aging which lead to cognitive decline but rather to their energy availability (and metabolism)[19]. Enough of all this science, the point is made! Let us look into what really concerns us — the good old Minni!

Oðin's Raven Munnin
And the Minni

We discussed the Grimnismal in 'The Spirit of Húnir Awakens (Part 1)' where, Oðin reveals that Hugin and Munin fly each day around the Midgard (Earth) and that he fears their loss. He fears the loss of Munin more than that of Hugin[20]. The importance of Munin and the greater fear Oðin has towards its potential loss is much more significant, even bordering the catastrophic. It is time to look at just why this is the case. It is not simply due to the fear of losing one's memory at the onset of old age. Old age is a human concept. A divine being who is also a shapeshifter can adopt any age he pleases so entering into this discussion is nonsensical at the core. Instead by looking at the functions of the Minni and how memory relates to various realities, we can see why there is such great value in it.

For the Gods and Goddesses, the Minni is of critical importance because they have no Fylgja. There is no inherited memory passed down to the next generation because this process does not apply to those who live eternally. A kin-Fylgja and Ætt -Fylgja most certainly would, but the personal Fylgja would not. It is simply a redundancy they no longer need at their current point in evolution.

That aside, the Minni plays a far more immediate and important role. We have seen how essential memories are when shifting across different realities and serve as links in between modes of awareness. Additionally, we will look below into how memories serve to unlock or rather re-connect with skills and abilities flowing through us — their potential is downright phenomenal. When looking at these few initial uses, you will see that it is actually a key to power itself. This is why Oðin is terrified of losing his Minni. He would instantly lose his ability to unlock the powers which are held within his memories. It is not only power which is in question here but also the references-coordinates of all the realities and all the places within each of those realities that you have ever visited which are accessible through the Minni and its memory functions. Can you imagine just how petrifying the thought of losing all that would be to the one God who went to extreme lengths just to acquire knowledge and wisdom in the Nine Worlds? Such loss would cause a loss of ability to shift into those worlds or precise known locations, to being able to access powers which requirement memory in addition to forgetting what one already knows. He would be in effect losing pretty much his very Self. Divine beings can reinvent themselves or re-create themselves but having to start from scratch after having lived since the beginning is a most terrifying thought indeed.

Minni Ale
Mystery of the Sumbl

One of the most prominent and well documented rituals in Norse culture was that of the drinking ale (termed the 'Sumbl') in remembrance of their Ancestors or the Gods. Its significance was even more striking due to the fact that, in those times, our ancestors had no set repertoire of rituals as most modern-day adaptations would suggest. They were few and far between. The Norse tradition is one of action. Even the Seidr practice of using a 'high seat' was not really a ritual but was more about giving the seat of authority as a sign of respect to the visiting Völva, who could do her work with or without the so called 'high seat'.

The term minni meaning "remembrance or memory" was used for ritual drinking dedicated to the remembrance of the gods. Terms used in this context, both in the Eddaic poems and in the Sagas, include minnis-öl "memory-ale", minnis-horn "memory-horn", minnis-full "memory-cup" and minni-sveig "memory-draught".

The Olafssaga (part of the Heimskringla[21], known as the Old Norse Kings' Sagas) uses the phrase minniöl signôð âsom meaning "they dedicated memory-ale to the æsir". "Memory-cups" dedicated to individual Gods are also named Oðins full, Niarðar full, Freys full etc[22]. The custom was continued uninterrupted by Christianization after which minni drunk to Christ, Mary and the saints.[23]

What we see is a strong importance attached to the process of remembering. In light of the information we have looked at so far with respect to the Minni, it is understandable why this is the case. However, the Minni Ale has far deeper mysteries to share, some which are going to have to be dealt with elsewhere. Let us say for now that the interlinking of memory and the events of life experience to which those memories point are essentially sent up to Ásgarðr during the drinking of the Minni Ale and some are shared with the Earth when its liquids are spilt into the ground. It is an exchange of accounts of awareness across the realities or worlds with the essence of Midgard and Ásgarðr. In return, the flow of awareness of those involved is increased, as well as the flow of life force from Midgard. What you have is a direct application of the mysteries of the Irminsul Pillar, the upwards and downwards flow of memory, events, knowledge, energy and even awareness.

Many have readopted this practice although they do not know how to make it work. Others have fused it with the Anglo-Saxon symbel. The former serves the purpose of swearing of oaths and bringing the community together around the chieftain's table as it is passed around. The older version of this ritual was, on the other hand, typically the domain of the priesthood and carried out in temples or sacred spaces as outlined in Heimskringla (Hakon the Good Saga) where goblets dedicated to the gods were used in addition to the minni one:

"And first Odin's goblet was emptied for victory and power to his king; thereafter, Njörd's and Freyja's goblets for peace and a good season. Then it was the custom of many to empty the bragafull; and then the guests emptied a goblet to the memory of departed friends, called the minni ['remembrance'].[24]"

As you can see from Snorri's account, the Sumbl provided a type of return power from the Gods themselves. In order to gain any actual benefit, something has to be sacrificed or gifted in exchange for a return gift. Without this component active, it would be ineffective. And just 'gifting' the ale itself is pointless since that does not even hold enough power to reach even the next level of reality, let alone all the way 'up' to Ásgarðr itself. Nor will it contain what it was originally meant to contain.

Now instead of tearing apart the half-lacking modern adaptations, let us look at how we can actually make it work. There are essentially two ways. The first was used by the rune masters of old and involves a set specific Galdr formula. Since revealing of this formulae has been expressly forbidden by Oðin himself, we are going to look at the second method. It is just as effective but involves a little more work and has a far more limited scope. In other words, you can use

125

this for yourself and maybe one or two individuals but not for a whole clan or assembly of people.

Start off by getting a drinking horn or a cup which you will ONLY use for this purpose. Then you will need to get your favourite alcohol. Most would opt for beer but that is by far the worst choice. Our ancestors used mead. Having selected your drink of choice, sit down and hold the cup or horn in both hands.

Do the practice of stirring the Minni (see Minni Enhancement and Amplification below). Once you have the Minni sitting on your head, send it the impulse or intent that you would like to spill a COPY of your life experiences into the drink and use it as a sacrifice to your Ancestors or the Gods and so forth. Here, we separate life experiences from the life force of our beings. It will understand what to do. Then simply intone the ᚠ Óss (Ansuz) rune (or do so via High Galdr) followed by the ◇ Ing (Ingwaz) and ᛒ Bjarkan (Berkano) runes. As you do, recall as vividly as possible what you want to send over — the more minute the detail, the better! With each exhale, breathe into the liquid within your horn or cup, intending to transfer the memories into the liquid. Because energy is attached to both the breath and the memories you are transferring, you will after a while see that energy pool or feel a slight vibration building up. When you have completed this process, will or intend the Minni to remerge into your brain. As it settles, you will be holding a cup full of mead imbued with personal life experience records.

The last thing you need to do is to offer it up to whomever you want with the intent that it is gifted

Sumbl - Memory Ale
& Drinking Horn Practice

to them. Wait a few seconds in silence and then gradually take little sips from the liquid. If you are sensitive to energy flow, you might feel an upwards and downwards flow as the gift is received and a counter-gift is made. If you do not feel it, no need to despair as it might be just a case of you not sensing it rather than it not happening! Watch your body and energy body reactions to the drinking closely as that is where you will potentially notice things taking place. Energy body (Hamr) awareness is likely to stir first, then a shift in actual mental awareness. It is a little different for each individual, however.

Quick Steps

1. Get hold of a drinking horn or a cup/mug you will only use for this purpose.
2. Select your favourite alcohol to use (except beer — that should be avoided at ALL costs).
3. Practice stirring the Minni into action until it sits on your head or left shoulder.
4. Focus on the Minni and send it the intent that you want it to spill a COPY of your life experiences into the liquid in your cup or drinking horn as a sacrifice to your ancestors or the Gods. No need to worry about how this is done the Minni knows and there is no need to overburden the conscious mind with it.
5. Then chant (or use High Galdr for) the runes: ◇ Ing (Ingwaz) and ᛒ Bjarkan (Berkano).
6. As you are chanting your runes recall as vividly as possible the memories you want to send over, the more detailed and clear the recall the better. As you breathe out, visualise the breath as it carries over the

energy and memories in a stream into the liquid.

7. Repeat 5 and 6 for each and every memory you want to send out. When done, you will feel the liquid vibrating with energy.

8. Intend the Minni to remerge in your brain. This will lock the memories into the liquid.

9. Spend a few moments in silence intending that this offering flows to the ancestors or the gods.

10. Drink of it with solemn thought on what is being offered and feeling the connection to whomever you offered it.

Minni Enhancement & Amplification

As discussed above in Memory and Energy, energy is key and the more energy the easier to remember and the more detail we will recall. This runs very true of the non-physical parts of the Self. You can use it as a gauge of energy availability simply by observing your recall of dreams and their details, vividness when you try to remember them. The better and easier this is the more energy you have in your energy stores. The less clear and the more difficulty you have or if you do not remember them at all this should be used as a warning sign that you are running critically low on energy. In this case immediately go and fill your Hamingja[25].

What we are going to look at now is how to increase the Minni's energy, think of it as a specialised memory energy. Because we are unable to produce the Mead of Memory as of yet we need to do it the good old-fashioned way with the runes instead. It is just as effective but much more work. Seeing as we are training and working on our skills and abilities the more work is what we actually want anyway.

Increasing physical energy for daily life is a big problem because as soon as you try to use any rune or energy and directly flood the brain with it you are causing fundamental changes in its function and structures which are impossible to dose correctly. There are only two runic formulae and a handful of runes we can safely use on the brain without running the risk of unforeseen consequences or introducing potentially long-term damage. Instead what we are going to do is amplify the energy of the Minni itself which we can do safely and let it spill over the additional energy in a safe manner as agreed by it and the cellular intelligence of our brains. We will cover this intelligence in greater detail at a later point in time. The practice is very similar to the one we used for the mind-reasoning (Hugr) with one key exception, the Minni is not suited to be a carrier of conscious awareness so we do not transfer our awareness into it as we do with the Hugr.

In order to stir the Minni into greater activity, you will need to go into a slight trance, either by siting with legs comfortable and hands on the respective leg. Do not cross the legs nor the hands. Sitting in a chair with back support and legs down is the best for energy flow. Relax, let go of all the tension, take a few breaths if needed and focus on relaxing! Let go of all the worries, fears, to do lists and so forth. Simply allow the world to fade from your awareness for the next 20 minutes. It need not even exist to your perceptions since it is not relevant. Next, focus on your thoughts simply observe them whilst your mind stills. Ignore the thoughts which pop into mind. As you do, you will notice that they do so less often. There is more time in between each thought that comes to mind. This is a sign of mild trance. Or if you have become skilled at the trance dance (outlined in the advanced section below), use that instead!

The next step involves focusing on the frontal cortex part of your brain. Simply think inside the forehead region. Once you get a feel for it, you should notice a mild pressure there. Then do exactly the same focus stage but on the whole of the right side of the brain. Wait until the pressure surfaces here too.

This is where we are going to differ from the Hugr practice in a significant fashion. It is vitally important you do not confuse the two or you will 'annoy' the Minni, creating a disharmony in between it, the Hugr and your consciousness.

What you will be doing at this point is intending (or willing if you are not skilled with intent yet), the Minni to surface. Very much like with the Hugr, it will rise out of those brain regions as a semi-solid energy body in the shape of a Raven but this time it will have a slight greenish glow to it. The more intense its glow, the more energy it has available. At all costs, do not try to imagine it all glowing and bright just to make it seem as if it is highly energised. That is NOT what we want. Allow it to manifest on its own. All you need to do when working with the Minni is send it an impulse or intent and let it do things the way it wants to. That is how female energy works — you seed it with impulse and it does its own thing. Avoid at all costs attempts to micro-manage it. This works on the male counterpart (the Hugr), but not on the Minni. All you will achieve in doing so is annoying it and causing resistance.

133

Should that occur, the only way forward is to either stop the practice altogether and try another day or to force it by imposition of will (which is the male over-powering female principle at play). Doing that when dealing with the Self and in this case the Minni, a very independent part of it, is a very very bad idea (unlike what we will do with the shadow (Sal) — well if you are a male you will do). More on that later.

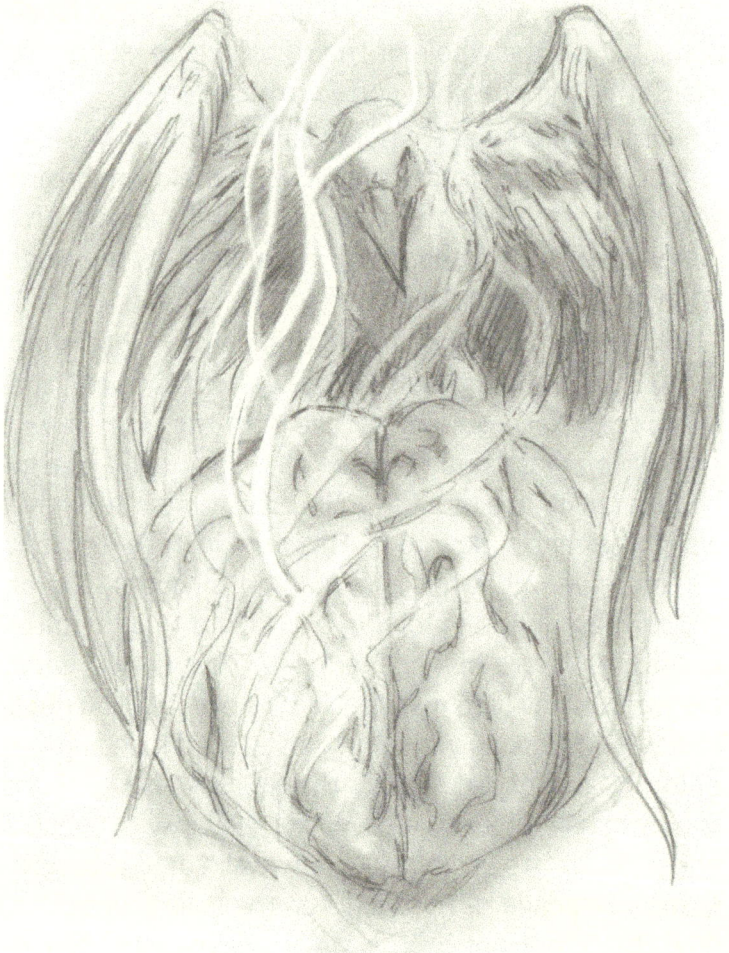

Minni Raven Rising From Brain

As it rises up from the brain in its energetic form and stands on your head, send out a thought or impulse of gratitude or appreciation. You will never go wrong with a 'thank you' for all its hard work (especially when dealing with a direct feminine manifestation). It might acknowledge your intent or it might not, but be genuine in your motivation. Whether it does or not is not important, so do not expect it or go looking for it. Just let things flow.

Once it has surfaced, chant the rune ᛒ Bjarkan (Berkano) or use High Galdr for it. See its deep green energy flood all the space about you. Feel its earthly solidity and energy everywhere and hear its name echoing in your mind. Then slowly pull the energy into the Minni itself. Be open to impression from it or, if you have mental sight developed, watch it. If there is any sign of discomfort or resistance, dissolve the runic energy and just sit there for a few moments before willing (or intending) it to remerge (or sink if you prefer) into your brain. If it has accepted the charge, it will start to hum, which is typically subtle. If you have keen senses, however, you will not fail to hear it. Its energy glow will intensify as well. Observe and sense it for as long as you wish and then gradually end the practice as described.

Quick Steps

1. Sit in the usual position and relax, allowing the world to fade from your awareness (or go into trance using the trance dance practice).
2. Silence your mind or at least still the onslau-

ght of thoughts.

3. Focus on the frontal cortex part of your brain (the front region just behind your nose). Then focus on the whole right side of your brain. Keep the focus up until you feel a slight pressure or tension.

4. Do not confuse the Hugr way of doing this with what you are going to be doing now or it will create disharmony in-between the two.

5. Like with the Hugr, the Minni will rise from those two brain regions as a surfacing energy pool which gradually takes on the shape of a raven. It will have a greenish glow. Do not force it to manifest. Just simply intend or will it and allow it to do so on its own.

6. At all costs avoid trying to direct things consciously with the Minni.

7. Send out an intent or impulse of gratitude to it, a simple token of appreciation is all that is needed.

8. When it has completely surfaced, chant the rune ᛒ Bjarkan (Berkano) and allow its deep heavy green energy to flood all of the space around you.

9. Pull all that ᛒ Bjarkan (Berkano) energy into the Minni.

10. Silently observe how the Minni reacts and get a sense of whatever impressions you get from it. If there is any sign of resistance or discomfort, stop immediately.

11. If all goes smoothly and the additional

energy is taken by the Minni, you will notice a type of vibration or a hum if you are sensitive to it. If all goes well, simply proceed.

12. Send the intent or impulse to the Minni to remerge and settle down in the brain regions that it came from.

What this will do is amplify the energy and seed matter for the Minni. It will also start the slow and gradual process of bringing the Minni closer to conscious awareness, as direct exchange of energy fused the parts together.

Minni & Hugr Raven Fusion
Mind Raven of Odin Takes Flight

Once your Minni and your Hugr have been sufficiently strengthened, it is time to use them in sync. Please be patient with this as it is a little 'fiddly' and can take a while for those two parts of the Self to understand and comply with what we will be asking them to do. So delicate slow progress here is warranted!

Start by doing the Setting the Hugr Raven to Flight. Once you are in the Hugr Raven, split your awareness into two. You have to be able to be aware of both being within your brain and perceive from it as well as from within the Hugr. Your perceptions have to flow from both. This might take a little practice so be patient and preserve with it. You will need to get a good solid footing in this dual awareness mode. For the observant ones you will notice that the perceptions are dual but the awareness is actually split rather than doubled. In all cases you should end up perceiving yourself both within the Raven and within your brain.

Having reached this point, perform the Minni Enhancement practice (the first part). Do NOT use the rune here. When you have the Minni Raven formed on top of your head, float right next to it from within the Hugr raven. You can now shift your full awareness back into the Hugr (you only need it split to be able to do the stirring into activity of the Minni raven).

This is where the tricky part begins. From within the Hugr Raven mentally chant the ᛞ Dagur (Dagaz) rune or better yet use High Galdr to do so. Visualise the rune between the two ravens. Intend the energy to flow from the Hugr to the Minni and back again. Study the shape of the rune and see how it flows. Let the energy flow exactly like that while the Hugr and Minni are at the sides of the rune. Allow the flow to start nice and soft, sending the impulse of harmony and coming together towards the Minni. It should respond. It you do not get anything back from it this time, end the practice. Otherwise continue. Gradually, and here VERY gradually is the key, increase the strength and speed of the flow. Allow things to progress. As the increase occurs, it will start to pull the Hugr Raven (you still inside it) and the Minni closer and closer to each other. Eventually the ᛞ Dagur (Dagaz) energy will start to become more compact as it intensifies. As it does, you and the Minni Raven will start to merge.

What we experience during such a merge cannot be put in words because it is very individual. Some describe this merging as a hyper-activation of their thinking, others experience it as a type of ecstasy. Whatever emotions flow through you, just let them flow, DO NOT get carried away by them. Whatever it is, do not let the experience carry you. You need careful, precise control of your reactions and constant awareness of how the Minni is reacting. Loss of concentration even for a split fraction of a second will tear you both apart, fracturing the merger. Such an occurrence will typically set you back for weeks, if not months. If all goes well, you will eventually end up merged with the Minni, in effect having a Hugr-Minni united Raven which can not only carry your conscious awareness but also carry with it perfect memory (as close to perfect as you can get without the energy body (Hamr)).

A word of caution here: you will get flooded with memories of all types and times. You need an iron will to avoid getting carried away in the flood. Remember that control is the key. Avoid focussing in on any specific memory, as that is not your goal here. Just let them pass by as if they were insignificant.

Now that you have a singular Raven form resulting from the merger of both the Hugr and Minni, you can proceed to take flight in what is a fully fledged Mind Raven. As you work through the Mind Raven, you will be able to do the same type of observations as you did in the Hugr Raven. The main difference here is that memory of what you observe and the detail with which you make those observations will be amplified tremendously. Always be careful and cautious to maintain harmony within the Mind Raven, however. When you feel resistance, take that as a warning against doing whatever you had planned to do. When directing impulses to it, remember it also contains the Minni and you should observe the rules of communication with it at all times. This is both an adaptation and learning practice. It takes time and practice but is well worth every ounce of effort you put into it.

Mind Raven Taking Flight
(produced by merging of the Hugr & Minni Ravens)

When doing this practice first time round, it is best to get to the point where you are in the merged Raven and just wait there for a while. This allows those parts of your Self to get accustomed to your awareness being there and being in direct control. This is an especially strange thing for the Minni which not only has never been subject to your conscious interaction(s) but is not suited to be a host or carrier of consciousness in the first place.

In order to end the practice, simply sink the merged raven back into the brain, allowing the energies and forms to spill over it. They will naturally adapt to their host areas without any need for you to get involved. They will also remain more merged than they ever were. Regular work with the Mind Raven will eventually result in full merger of the Hugr and Minni. Once that takes place, you can proceed to taking the final step in full mental level Self unification using specific runic formulae for this. We will look at those at a later time. For the time being, we need to initiate this merging and get you used to being within the Mind Raven before you can start unleashing Galdr from it.

Quick Steps

1. Start with Setting the Hugr raven to flight.
2. Once you are in the Hugr Raven, split your awareness into two. You have to be able to be aware of both being within your brain and perceive from it as well as from within the Hugr.
3. Whilst keeping your awareness and perceptions

in the Hugr going, from your brain's perspective do the Minni Enhancement practice up to the point where you have the Minni Raven out. Float from within the Hugr raven towards the Minni raven.

4. Shift all your awareness back into the Hugr Raven (you are vacating the brain of all awareness and hence perception).

5. From within the Hugr Raven (where your full awareness should be rooted now), mentally chant (or use High Galdr) the rune ᛗ Dagur (Dagaz). Visualise the rune between the two Ravens and see the energy flow from the one into the other in the form of the rune. As it passes through the Hugr raven, feel it pulling you in the direction of the Minni Raven.

6. Allow the flow and the pull to get stronger and stronger. As it does, the two ravens will keep moving towards each other until they touch and then start to merge. When they do, feel, see and sense them fusing into each other, until eventually they are fully merged and form a single Raven: the Mind Raven.

7. All sorts of reactions and impressions, memories and feelings will surface and flow through your perception. Do not react but just observe them and allow them to flow.

8. Get used to this new form of conscious awareness with enhanced perceptions and memory.

9. Repeat steps 1 to 8 until they become simple to do and you get used to being within the

Mind Raven and the new type of perceptive skills you will have gained.

10. When you are familiar with it, it is time to take flight in the Mind Raven.

11. In order to end the practice simply glide back into the brain allowing its energy to diffuse within the brain. There is no need to split into the individual ravens they will do so automatically.

12. Take a few deep breaths and let your awareness to switch back to the usual normal function.

One of the big side effects that you will notice as you practice this is that your memory improves dramatically. Not only that, but your ability to carry or bridge memories form trance states and other modes of awareness to your normal daily awareness amplifies to such an extent that it will eventually match the one you use in daily life. In other words, there will be no effort or difficulty in bridging the enhanced states of awareness and the normal one, nor will there be any challenges in recalling what happened or using the information gained in between them.

HEALING VIA MEMORIES

Anyone who has ever either been to or talked to a councillor will tell you that they make their patients live through painful memories in order to help them process them. Sometimes it works, other times not. That method is indeed close to correct but as usual when something is only half-applied accurately, it produces only half the results.

The problem with simply recalling, reliving, or talking about a traumatic experience is that the patient reconnects to the memory, and thereby reconnects to the energies, pains and trauma. This is then talked about in order to diffuse the energetic concentration. With a good practitioner, the talking part will temporarily diffuse the dynamics behind the event and alleviate the effects unleashed by it. However, if the patient is not able to disconnect from it effectively and the memory keeps coming back to mind, the energetic charge can grow exponentially. Typically, when this occurs drugs are the modern day solution.

This pitfall can be avoided simply by applying the full technique properly which will not only diffuse the energy attached to the traumatic experience and associated events but will also disconnect the patient from the entire experience. It will also allow him to reclaim his own energy which was spilt during the trauma (remember Megin from The Breath of Oðin Awaken[26]?).

You can detach yourself from it by simply doing the 'Reclaiming your Energy' and / or 'Memory Ale' practices by focussing on the traumatic event and visualising yourself re-experiencing it, as this will transfer it all as experiential essence to the Fylgja. Having done this, you will not only feel 'free' of the experience but also stronger (because you have reclaimed the energy spilt during the events attached to it).

Naturally, this can be done with not only traumatic experiences but with ANY experience. High stress ones are excellent subjects for this, as are very exciting ones, too. Include both good and bad ones. Why? Because those drain just as much Megin and energy as the bad ones do. Actually, if precision is required, some good experiences can drain far more than bad ones because we get more attached to the good ones and long for more of them or for them to continue. They are a massive drain on the systems and fracture the Self once it has sufficiently weakened. Ever wondered why two people in 'love' end up being so dependent on each other? Well now you know. A fractured Self will seek another to bond with another in order to sustain itself. The initial euphoric state runs out of energy very fast and then the drain commences; so does the possessiveness, jealousy, clinging behaviours and so forth. All these need to be processed and released, otherwise the Spirit (Óðr) cannot fly free.

Remember the Minni is a raven sitting on Oðin's shoulder. It is also sent to fly over the Nine Worlds to survey for him. It is not chained or wingless!

MEMORIES TO UNLEASH INNER POTENTIAL & POWER

During their schooling, many students struggle with exams due to the fear that they will lack the necessary recall capabilities when the time comes. A simple Minni recall trick can help with scoring top marks in all exams. This practice is also used to gain access to power points in our memory records.

Let us cover the mechanical recall used in exams first and foremost. The technique is shockingly simple. Do your revision in the same place each and every time you do. Do the actual studying in that same place as well. By repeated use of a space for a given purpose, the energetic imprint of that purpose is made upon the space around us AND within us. They harmonise energetically. This is a vital key to grasp and it will be covered in great depth when looking at quantum consciousness. There is nothing to do in order to make this spacial and personal imprint or harmonisation, as they happen automatically. It is a side-effect of being an energy being.

On the day of the examination, simply take a deep breath and relax. Visualise yourself as vividly as possible as sitting in the place in which you did your studying and revision. Using the ᛟ Óðal (Othala) rune, chant it mentally (in your head only) and feel its power flood you and the immediate space around you, forming an energetic bubble with you in its centre. Then see the rune under your chair or under your feet if you are using this whilst standing. All around you, keep the visualisation of the place in which you did your study and revision. Stick to this no matter what. If you get distracted and become aware of the examination room, shift back to the place of study the very next instant. You should completely ignore the examination room, all the people within it, and everything else. Simply focus on your paper and each time you can, re-affirm your visualised space. The ᛟ Óðal (Othala) energies will serve to temporarily ground you there. This synchronises you both in the study mode you were in when studying, makes your memories from then accessible in the NOW and re-harmonises you to the energy patterns you established while studying and revising. With practice, effortless recall can be achieved.

Always remember when finished to make the rune reabsorb the energy it was radiating and then fade away from your awareness.

The main reason for this technique to be presented here is, of course, not to assist with revision, albeit all those studying will greatly appreciate it. The main reason is to outline it in order to enable you to use it for mysticism. Some places are conducive to trance states, expansion of awareness and so forth. All your practices should be done in the same space over and over again whenever possible. This will make the area conducive to mystical energies and make crossing the boundaries of the limitations of standard awareness to higher forms easier. All you need to do then to unleash the higher perceptions is to visualise yourself in that place and apply the same technique. You will notice that reconnecting with those abilities, states of being and the general flow of consciousness is much easier, if not instant. Master this technique well. It will be used to a much greater extent later on when you start to establish personal spaces in the other Nine Worlds and rune streams.

TAPPING INTO MEMORIES OF
PERSONAL POWER

When practicing, there will be points in time when you experience great rushes of power. If done correctly, even the work from 'The Breath of Oðin Awakens'[27] will provide such direct experiences from the outset. Feelings such as being on top of the world, having a flow of intense pure power through your body, feeling the energy body (Hamr) vibrating with life, sensing the universe flow through you, feeling like the incarnation of the full power of a rune stream and so forth are all experiences you should keep an eye out for AND make a good mental solid note of. When they occur, experience them fully. Allow all the sensations of these experiences to flow through every pore of your very being. Make mental note of them and every facet of them AND send out the thought to both your Minni and Fylgja to make you remember them. A simple thought is all that is needed, as the entire process is automatic. The addition of a directing thought creates a stronger link between the Hugr and the Minni in respect of that memory. This is important for life long recall. When working from the standard mode of awareness, recall is not guaranteed unlike how memories work in enhanced state of awareness. In those enhanced states they are automatically forever written into your very being always influencing and impacting never truly forgotten.

Having a few of those memories under your belt, it is time to put them to some good proper use! Please do note that if you are doing this in order to access such states of being whilst working with the other realities or Nine Worlds, this technique needs to be avoided. There is another one which will be covered later on which is used for that, as there you will need to bridge awareness of the reality before connecting with the required state. A bit more work is needed before going into that much depth.

Whether you wish to do this in a logically structured manner or a more intuitive one is entirely up to you. You are simply going to select three memories of such states of power and use those. Typically, some prefer to pre-select them before starting whilst others select the first and let their intuition carry them from there. It makes no difference which selection method is used.

Start by mentally uttering the ᚠ Óss (Ansuz) rune calling forth its energy to flood you. Uttering them out loud will cause a different effect and render these practices ineffective. The ᚠ Óss (Ansuz) energies are dark blue and light to the touch. Make sure they are constantly free flowing around you, through you and about you. They are never static but rather like a wind, a flow of air. These are the energies of freedom and remove the fetters of social conditioning from our minds.

Once you have established the mental currents of ᚠ Óss (Ansuz), mentally chant the ᛒ Bjarkan (Berkano) rune, adding its energy to this flowing current and focus on the Minni activating (note: you are not separating it, but causing an activation of its functions whilst it is still in the brain). This will send it into what can best be described as a graceful frenzy. Its activity will increase to the point where keeping track of it even in visualisations is so difficult that it ends up being totally pointless. Just let it do its thing and instead focus on the next rune.

Finally, mentally utter the ᛗ Dagur (Dagaz) rune. Here you have a choice: you can either visualise the rune in your chest, head, hips or under your feet. With the chest and head, only use it there if it does not cause too much pressure. If it does, stick to the hips or under feet. The reason for the multiple positions is that you can unleash the source of the incoming power from any of those positions. Some of you will have a specific affinity for one spot or the other and others will be able to use multiples, if not all. Still others yet might simply prefer it one way or another. Practice and see what feels right — remember, following your feeling here is key as that is a signal from the physical body (Lik) AND energy body (Hamr). Always listen to those feelings and impulses you receive from the body or energy body (Hamr) which surface during practices as they always have something important to communicate to you.

The ᛗ Dagur (Dagaz) energy is outflowing and expansive. For those of you who have worked with energies, you will easily notice the similarity it has to pure bluish light mixed with a vividly sparkling electric current. It is a very expansive energy. Once you feel the slight rush of mind and energy, it is time to get down to the fun work!

Start with the first memory of power and visualise yourself in it. You are doing the actual practice you originally did to induce that power rush, energy rush, sensations or whatever you are after. Feel it as if it was happening right now. Flood your mind with the memory. Flood your mind within the memory. Forget the body. Just engross yourself in the memory of power. Once you start to feel that same state of power rising in your body, will the ᛞ Dagur (Dagaz) energy to carry the energetic state over to you more and more. It will intensify until it is well established and you cannot tell whether this was induced from a memory or if it was induced by doing the entire practice right now. Will it to remain; a simple intending it to keep pulsating and not physically moving will enable you to maintain it. Then move onto the next memory and repeat. When that one has started flowing in, you will feel both types of energy rushing through you in a very disjointed manner. To our mental perceptions this is very confusing state. You are feeling the first flowing constantly, then the second which is completely separate. Your mind tries to interpret it which naturally it will fail to do. It then reasons through it by imposing a restriction on your perceptions to make it feel as if the one state switches to the other and back. In fact, they are both there but you are only momentarily perceiving the one then the other and so forth.

Add the third and final memory to this repeating the practice. We work in sets of three due to the natural disposition of trinities blending into each other.

If you really want to add further memories, there is nothing stopping you from doing so but it will rapidly overload your perceptions and the resulting energetic fusion will be less effective. Once you have three, things can get really confusing so the best way to deal with it is to let the experience flow and not try to reason anything at this point in time. Rather, just focus on just being the impartial observer and observe. To finish this off, mentally utter the rune ᛩ Vin (Wunjo) and feel its cooling, harmonising energy flood you. As it does, something fascinating occurs — all these separate states are united into one overriding state of power. Your mind will no longer flicker through each state in a rapid but distinct perception but will emerge. As they do, the qualities of all three will blend into one harmonious sensation. Enjoy it.

Quick Steps

1. Mentally chant the rune ᚠ Óss (Ansuz) and pull its dark blue light energy flowing around you as a flow of air and into you and then once again around you. This time, it never stays static or at rest but is always flowing in and out, through and throughout.
2. Now mentally chant the ᛒ Bjarkan (Berkano) rune adding its energy to the flowing current and will its energy to activate the Minni.
3. The next step involves a choice and it is suggested here to listen to the impulses coming from your body and / or your energy body. It is also a good idea to try them all

see which one works best or which one you are most comfortable with. You can either mentally chant the ᛗ Dagur (Dagaz) rune causing its energy to flow from either the head, chest, hips or under the feet. If you feel pressure or discomfort in head or disrupted breathing in chest, switch to one of the two positions in the lower body instead.

4. As the somewhat soft electric energy of ᛗ Dagur (Dagaz) is added to the current (from wherever you opted to have it flow in the body) you will notice a rush both in your energy body (Hamr) and your mind.

5. Start with the first memory of the practice you did and whose power you would like to recall. Allow all the details to flood you, all the images, the sensations, the emotions and state of mind you were in. You should fuse with the you in that memory as if it was happening right now.

6. You will feel the power or ability you were hoping to reconnect with rising. At that point will (or intend) the ᛗ Dagur (Dagaz) energy to carry that energetic state over to you in your current time (remember memories are the past not current, when you are remembering you are in effect projecting your awareness back to that point of reference in time).

7. Will the ability / power to remain within you and be accessible from this point onwards.

8. When ready move onto the next memory.

9. When done chant the ᚹ Vin (Wunjo) rune

feeling and intending its energy to harmonise the reconnected powers / abilities with the you now.

The power behind this is as real as it was when you initially did each practice but it is also combined. Use it and allow it to fade or funnel it into the Hamingja. Remember not to just leave it there or it will put a lot of energetic pressure on your system. You have summoned it forth for a reason so do something with it.

With practice, it becomes possible to simply use the ᚠ Óss (Ansuz) and ᚹ Vin (Wunjo) runes to very rapidly reconnect to states of power and bring them forth into the NOW as if they were caused through the full practices. At higher levels of proficiency, it is possible to do so within a matter of seconds. Take heed of this practice, as you will be using it extensively with High Galdr.

ACTIVE REMEMBERING

Having arrived at this point of our practical work it becomes possible to direct the Minni consciously in order to force remembering. Let us delve into this a little more. When you remember something spontaneously, you might later on forget the memory, or only recall it loosely. As time passes recall becomes more and more difficult. With 'active remembering' or if you prefer remembering as a result of expressing the intent to remember, the conscious mind directs the formation of a given memory. Such a memory will 'stick', in other words be hard wired and drive you to recall it.

All this involves is focusing on an event you want to remember and send the intent to your Minni. A simple command such as 'remember this', or 'I will remember this' directed at the Minni works wonders. Providing you have worked with the above practices on the Minni, this is all you should require. Now you will find that as soon as you want to recall the memory, it will be available in unusually vivid detail. Even if you do not consciously trigger the desire to recall, the memory will surface back on its own, in other words you are 'automatically or spontaneously remembering'.

To get even more control over this skill, you can fine tune the remembering trigger and / or intent. For instance, instead of just 'Remember this', you can use 'I will remember this until ...' add whatever condition you want there. You can also do something like 'I will remember this when I write my diary'. As soon as you sit down to write, the memories will come flooding back with better and better clarity and precision. **Always keep in mind that, when you are remembering, if your eyes shift to the left then you are imagining not remembering.** If they shift to the right, you are actually recalling. Use this to filter out any additional information you might be imagining into your actual recall.

Practice this quick method each time you can. We will look at how this can be extended to consciously carry memories from energy aware states to your normal awareness and vice versa.

IMAGINATION & MEMORY

When you imagine something, you are building an image of it in your mind. This is an action of the spirit (Óðr) via the Hugr and will automatically trigger the Minni into writing a record and create pointers to whatever has been imagined. Because this process is exactly the same when you are experiencing or observing something occurring. In those situations, the spirit (Óðr) via the mind-reason (Hugr) and sensory input looks at the event this in turn also triggers the Minni to start recording all that is seen. As you can see, the two are so similar that they are practically identical but not quite. This is all that is needed for a memory to be established, hence the confusion between real memories and what science terms 'false memories'. Realistically speaking, from an energy point of view there is no such thing as a 'false' memory. Even the imagined is experienced and is therefore as real to the spirit (Óðr) as an actual physical experience. In a recent study, Susumu Tonegawa, the Picower Professor of Biology and Neuroscience stated this fact in his findings:

> "Whether it's a false or genuine memory, the brain's neural mechanism underlying the recall of the memory is the same"[28]

and

> "This work has revealed striking similarities between remembering the past and imagining or simulating the future, including the finding that a common brain network underlies both memory and imagination."[29]

If in doubt, ask those who suffer from phobias and anxiety just how real their experiences get! They are often so real that they can completely paralyse those individuals. Actually, a very recent study into visual perceptions found that 'inferred' visual objects generated by the brain (in effect imagined object built on established logic rules) were treated as more reliable than objects seen in the real world[30].

As we have ve discussed above, when looking at the mental level of reality and how the thought-energy dynamics work, it is simple for all to understand how an imagined memory leads to a real one. The memory is recalled then thoughts associated with that memory stir. From their recall, the Hugr is once again activated and does its typical echoing of concepts out, eventually leading to more and more energy gathering around the recalled memory, whether imagined or real. Thus it leads down into the energetic side of reality and is hurdled towards manifestation. This is why we can use imagination, through the medium of memory, to access realities and energies we never actually experienced before. If we did experience them then that would only accelerate the process. The speed of shift from memory to reality is determined solely on the strength of the memory. One which has been recalled many times will be stronger than a new one, hence why the recall of an actual experience or an energy we have had contact with will be faster to lead back to it.

We will look at how this gives us practically unlimited potential to expand awareness and perceptions, limited only by the scope of our spirit (Óðr) which can be stretched beyond anything the average person on the street would ever dream. This expansion of potential is also an important key when looking at Fylgja memories left by the ancestral member who was our previous Self. Additionally, the kin-Fylgja holding ancestral memories spanning countless centuries of invaluable knowledge and memories provides an additional 'store' waiting to be accessed once again (especially for the eldest male of the family line).

Powers of ᛒ, ᛏ, ᚠ and ◇ Runes

When working with memories, these four runes have an important dynamic and deep impact regardless of what is being done with their energies. This is primarily due to their function on the Minni. Let us take a quick look at those since they are being used in the above given practice.

ᛒ Bjarkan (Berkano) is the rune of the Minni. No matter what we do with its energy, it will always strengthen the Minni and all its functions. It does this due not only to its relationship with that part of the Self but with memory itself. Since memories are energetic seeds or imprints of events and experiences, ᛒ Bjarkan (Berkano) will always seek to mature them to full fruition. It does this in different ways depending on the type and use of the given memory but it will always bring it closer to fruition.

ᛏ Týr (Tiwaz) is a rather special rune in terms of the Minni. Its job is to record references to the places where memories are located in the energy body and the auric field. Upon death, it will transfer all those along with the actual memories to the Fylgja, as they become ancestral memories preserved for the next generation. This requires often great strife because on quite a few occasions, the Self runs across experiences that it does not want to remember, memories it refuses to acknowledge, memories it does not want to give up and, upon death, it does not want to let go. ↑ Týr (Tiwaz) is the runic energy which supports the functions of the Minni in its memory housekeeping, even if it means ripping them out of the Self by force and diminishing it for the sake of future generations.

ᚠ Óss (Ansuz) breaks the shackles of the mind and sets us free by giving it wings! ᚠ Óss (Ansuz) and memory have a love-hate relationship. When the mind and spirit (Óðr) are capable, they work hand-in-hand with memory by ensuring a smooth transition from one state of mind (and hence remembering) to another. When they do not, the saying 'fleeting memory' becomes all too true and even trying to remember something which occurs might seem like an impossible task. Yet those energies coil back on themselves and enable the mind to set flight and re-enter those elevated states of consciousness, thereby re-accessing those very memories as current.

◇ Ing (Ingwaz) is a key runic energy when it comes to both the Minni and memories themselves. It is often the loss of this energy which leads to memory problems. It enables the solidification and consolidation of memories in their appropriate place and the formation of the references pointing to them both on the energetic and in the neurological brain networks. It in effect, locks the essence of experiences along with the memories which gave rise to it for later recall.

It is wise to keep in mind these general effects of those specific four runes in terms of the Minni and memory. Even when used for something completely different or unrelated on the mental level of the Self, these effects will take place regardless of what you use the runic energy for.

FORMATION IN SPIRIT

The Art of Visualisation

Everything we do in Norse Mysticism is calculated to produce specific results, so the term 'art' should be avoided when referring to it. This rule can be a little more relaxed, however, when it comes down to visualisations. There are certain tricks to it but ultimately speaking, visualisation is more of a learnt art than a calculated scientific process with a specific result.

Most will wonder why even enter into discussions relating to visualisation in the first place. Surely everyone can visualise? Well, yes and no. Some people completely lack the ability to form mental imagery but that is mostly due to an extremely rare brain defect affecting a handful of individuals globally. Everyone else does have the ability to form mental imagery. Visualisation, however, is not limited to mental imagery. It should include all the senses as well as 'sensing' itself. Hence even if you are one of those rare people who cannot visualise, you can do so using your other senses.

Forming visualisations brings all the senses together, so whatever you are visualising must include seeing (imagery), hearing (sound), sensations (feeling), smelling (odour) and, if possible, tasting. To these we are going to add sensing. Most think that because the term visualisation is composed of 'visual' and '-isation', it out of necessity requires only the visual imagery components or visual processes. This is why so many visualisations actually fail to produce any actual results. One sense alone does not have sufficient empowering effects to solidify whatever it is you are visualising. The senses of taste and smell can be very tricky but remember young children explore the world (initially) by putting everything in their mouths thereby touching and tasting things. You need to do the same whenever possible. Involve ALL your senses.

Once all five senses are involved, you will need to add sensing itself, which as we discussed before is the sense of the spirit. Unless you can spiritually 'read' or 'sense' whatever it is you are visualising, then it simply does not exist.

One important thing to keep in mind is that the primary five senses are a manifestation of touch. When you see, what is actually happening is your eyes are touching the light that objects and people reflect. If they absorbed it, you would see them as a black object). As the light touches your eyes' corona, it triggers electrical impulses in the brain which are interpreted as upside down images. The brain inverses them for you, which incidentally confuses those who start to project out of their bodies to no end since the brain no longer does this for them. A similar thing occurs with all the other senses. Hearing occurs when sound waves touch your inner ears, feeling when your skin makes contact with something or someone, smell when odour touches receptors in the nasal passages and tasting involves a multitude of touch-based inputs, as outlined below:

"But what is taste actually? What happens in our body that enables us to perceive flavor? The chemical substance responsible for the taste is freed in the mouth and comes into contact with a nerve cell. It activates the cell by changing specific proteins in the wall of the sensory cell. This change causes the sensory cell to transmit messenger substances, which in turn activate further nerve cells. These nerve cells then pass information for a particular perception of flavor on to the brain [...]

What is generally categorized as "taste" is basically a bundle of different sensations: it is not only the qualities of taste perceived by the tongue, but also the smell, texture and temperature of a meal that are important. The "coloring" of a taste happens through the nose. Only after taste is combined with smell is a food's flavor produced. If the sense of smell is impaired, by a stuffy nose for instance, perception of taste is usually dulled as well."[31]

In other words, taste is a product of multiple manifestations of touch. Pure sensing works on this basis, too, when your Spirit (Óðr) touches energy, mental formations of concepts and abstractions and so forth. Ultimately, it is all one single sense manifesting in a number of different ways.

Now you can understand why involving all the senses will strengthen your visualisations. Instead of a single touch, that visualisation will be experiencing six of them at a time. Doing all of this in your visualisation technique will add energy to it and we have seen how energy plus thought leads to manifestation. Interestingly, the sixth rune in the first Ætt is < Kaun (Kenaz) which points to the concept of controlled (under will) fire (empowerment). Here we introduce a bit of runic numerology for you to consider!

Mastering visualisation requires one final step, and that is imbuing it with intent. Everything in Creation has purpose, directionality and energy. We have looked at how to imbue these visualisations with as much energy as possible, and the last stage of pushing that thought and energy combination into manifestation involved imbuing it with actual intent. Intent will give it purpose and, with the addition of purpose, it gains directionality.

Typically, with runic energy work we automatically imbue our visualisations with some intent. After all, there is a reason we are doing the visualising in the first place. Actual intent, however, will amplify this to unmeasurable levels. You have learnt the basics regarding the mystery of intent above. Use that skill or practice to imbue your visualisations with more intent. When we look at intent in the next work, you will just need to add that second layer to your visualisation to give them a lot of extra 'kick'. Mastering this is critically important because it will enable you to make rapid progress in your energy manipulation and usage abilities.

POSITIONING VISUALISATIONS

Most will wonder what on earth is meant by positioning visualisations. It becomes relevant only whilst visualising when in your physical body (Lik), energy body (Hamr) and/or shadow (Sal). So what is this positioning all about? In short, it has to do with how visualisations interact and are interpreted whilst you are in one of your bodies on the energetic level of reality (or the Self, for that matter). Let us put this right into context in order to avoid causing any confusion. When in your physical body on a daily basis, you see straight ahead of you and to a limited extend to the periphery of yourself (called the peripheral vision range). The eyes are receptive organs of the brain. Note the word 'receptive', which means they are receivers first and foremost. What happens when most people visualise? Typically, you would form your images in front of you out of sensory habit learned from sight. What this causes is you trying to see again, you are 'projecting' something by using a receiving mechanism. See the problem? It is like turning a power switch off and wondering why your computer is not on and working. The current is in the wrong position (off rather than on). The same happens when you try to project your field of vision to the front of you and its peripheral range. Anything you visualise, no matter how fantastic your visualisation skills are or how much detail you have put into it, no matter how powerful the intent imbued within it, if projected into your field of vision it will short-circuit and fail because this is how you receive environmental information on both the physical and the energetic. On the mental level of reality, there is no such thing as directionality and therefore it cannot short circuit. As soon as you force it to manifest on the energetic, however, directionality and shape come into play. By positioning the visualisation on the receptive area you are wasting all your hard work, time and energy. This is a big no-no!

The trick is to visualise or rather project your visualisation OUTSIDE of the range of vision or just on the border so that it is mostly outside but can have a little part crossing over into the field of vision. This applies to open eye visualisation AND closed eye ones. When you are doing them with eyes shut and staring at the black background of your closed eyelids ALWAYS make sure you are visualising outside of your field of vision because the eyes (and especially later on the energy body eyes) are still receiving information there. The only issue being that they are receiving blackness of the back of your eyelids but receiving nonetheless they are!

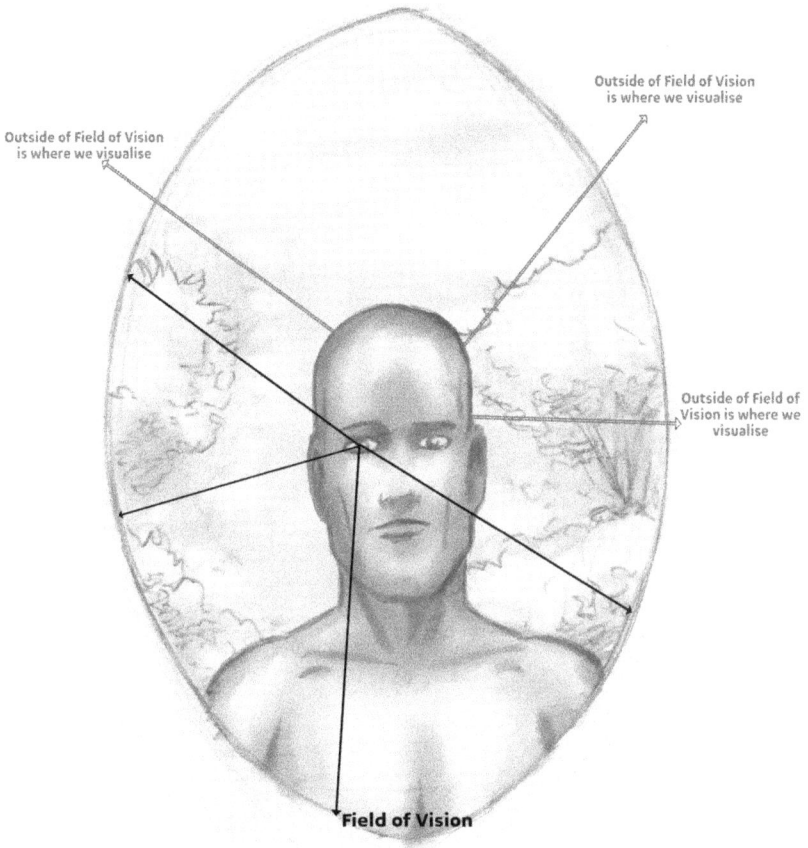

Outside of Field of Vision
is where we visualise

Outside of Field of Vision
is where we visualise

Outside of Field of Vision
is where we visualise

Outside of Field of
Vision is where we
visualise

Field of Vision

Visualisation Range
(showing how visualisation has to
be done outside of the field of vision)

As soon as you start visualising OUTSIDE of your field of vision, you are pushing your visualisations into energetic reality and, in time (depending on the amount of energy and strength of intent), into the densest parts thereof (in other words, the physical). This, ladies and gents, is the key to visualising! And the key to not failing. It is also the reason why, except in projections of Self, you always focus on being in vast

183

empty space all around you, and you visualise the runic energies all around you. Yes, some parts will hit the visual range but most will not!

VISUALISATION VS IMAGINATION

This is a topic of immense confusion because a lack of understand is usually present when comparing these two activities of the mind. There is imagination and imagination. Even more confused? Not to worry. There are different types of imagination. We most often we encounter is the first type when we try to recall something and imagine it instead. In other words, we imagine what we want to remember instead of the actual events as they happened. We have seen in 'The Spirit of Húnir Awakens (Part 1)'[32] how the brain fails to distinguish between a memory and an imaginary occurrence. The other form of imagination surfaces when we are wishing for something or desiring something, often during day dreaming and those endless 'what ifs' people have a habit of engaging in. Another manifestation of this type of imagination happens when we are driven by emotion. In this case, we imagine scenarios such as the perfect romantic outing or partner, how we will get revenge or how we will accomplish a much desired goal. The final type

of imagination we encounter happens when visualising, which we will call 'directed, willed imagination'.
Why is this different? Because it has purpose, function
and focus which the other types do not have. they
have wishful thinking or impulse reaction instead but
no 'dimensionality'.

When visualising, we are taking imagination and
making it an active tool of the mind controlled and
directed by our will. This gives it a dimensionality
which other forms of imagination do not naturally
have. In this way, it is something more than just imagination. Because the modern mind loves to dabble in
the 'but is it real' nonsense, let us look into that
right now and put the whole issue into our 'resolved'
box.

So is this type of imagination real? Yes, not as real
as a physical object by any stretch but it is real
nonetheless. Once you use willed and directed imagination, you are gathering into it all the hallmarks
of the things needed to manifest your desire from
the mental into the energetic levels. As more and
more energy, intent and, most importantly, thought
coalesces into whatever it is we have wilfully imagined,
it echoes out on the mental level and pulls more of
what is like it into itself, propelling it faster and faster
into a more tangible reality. In effect, you are using
imagination under willed direction to bridge things
into reality. Your energy body (Hamr), and even your
physical body (Lik), will eventually start reacting to it in
exactly the same way as it does with actual reality.

This is one of the most fascinating creative powers
of our minds — once unlocked wonders await! So stop
wasting your imagination. Seize them by your will and

direct them for your own evolution and benefit. Do not waste such an important ability.

Runically speaking, we see the ᚲ Kaun (Kenaz) rune once again in action here. The inspiration of ᚠ Óss (Ansuz) is directed by willed imagination (ᚱ Reið (Raidho)) into realisation (ᚲ Kaun (Kenaz)). By crossing the imagined-real point via exchange of energy and intent (ᚷ Gjöf (Gebo)) and harmonised (hence manifests) into actual reality (ᚹ Vin (Wunjo)) it thereafter becomes a part of it. We will look at these runic flows in a lot of detail. Using this rune combination, activating them one after the other, can provide you with assistance in speeding up such manifestations into actual reality.

RUNIC TRANCE
&
THE NORSE 'HOLY GRAIL'

Advanced: Mapping Expansion of Consciousness via Runes

It is time to take our understanding of the runes out of the typical usage and into a more universal one. In this case, we are going to look at how the runic energies relate to consciousness and, more specifically, to its evolution. By understanding how the runic energies are reflected within conscious awareness, we can easily determine what stage of development we are at, which rune plays the greatest role in our perceptive mechanisms and which ones we should be aiming for next. Sometimes it is impossible to pinpoint an exact rune or an exact stage of development. That is fine. Things on the mental level of the Self are in constant flux. In fact, it is the level of reality where such fluctuations will be the greatest and most pronounced. The archetypal level is as close to absolute as it can be and hence does not change. Rather, it manifests itself and re-manifests. This might appear as change to those who do not perceive that level of reality but in fact there is no change — just a differentiation in what is and what is not manifest and how it is manifest. The underlying essence of things at this level of reality is always the same. We just see different 'faces' or 'facets' of it.

We know that the runes themselves have been written and embedded by Oðin in all things made. Yet we also know that they pre-date the Gods and Goddesses. They were in existence and known to something or someone else before being communicated to Oðin. They are, for all intents and purposes, a universal (or cosmic) and dimensional set of tools. Due to their all-pervasiveness, they can be used to interpret consciousness itself.

It is important to keep in mind when reading through this that these stages described below are repeated in macro- as well as micro-cycles. In other words, consciousness first ascends through the 24 runic stages of development and then descends them, finally becoming them upon the final ascent. This process is hinted at by the final rune ᛟ Óðal (Othala) which points to the return to one's roots.

The whole process is fairly simple. One ascends the runes, taking physical consciousness up into the spiritual realms, then reverses the flow and works through the runes from ᛟ Óðal (Othala) to ᚠ Fé (Fehu), carrying down the spiritual to ground it back into the physical in order to finally ascend anew carrying up a merged physio-spiritual consciousness into the heights of cosmic consciousness.

The First Ætt

Before Creation was set into motion, there was stasis. Into stasis came motion. This is also true of consciousness until it awakens. The onset of forces of ᚠ Fé (Fehu) awaken it to activity. Typically causing an awakening into violent and undirected activity, activity for the simple sake of being active. This is the first awakening of consciousness into activity but still shrouded in confusion as it attempts to discover where and what it is as it orients itself to the reality around it. This initial activity sees a period of settling down as guided by forces of ᚢ Úr (Uruz). Consciousness has come to terms with its environment and has assessed its initial spark or flame.

ᚢ Úr (Uruz) signals a change in focus. It starts to settle down and turn inward. It is fed by experience and a type of digestive process within itself is initiated. This results in a degree of solidification. Self-identity gradually starts to shape under the influences of this rune. Perceptions of 'I' vs outer reality awakens. A degree of stability is seen by the manifestation of self-perception through the 'I'. Consciousness turns about and is able to intone 'I am', yet it does not know what it is, knowing only that it is.

Establishing the 'I' initiates the forces of ᚦ Þurs (Thurisaz) to surface. Consciousness has to defend this perception of Self because it is threatened by all that which is not 'I'. External stimulus is fought against as resistance to the 'I' is perceived for the first time and battled against. That which is not part of the 'I' is either taken as a threat or something which has to be brought in line with the 'I' or at least

193

reconciled with it. Here we have consciousness learning about adversity, the challenge being to learn and grow from its battles and develop an understanding of conflicts. This signals the manifestation of adversarial consciousness.

Having fought the battles of ᚦ Þurs (Thurisaz) and established the foothold of self-consciousness, the 'I' starts to realise what its own potential is and is not. It gains insight into what should be fought against and what battles should be avoided. At this point, consciousness is now able to take its next step.

Through the powers of ᚨ Óss (Ansuz), it now enters a state of bliss and elevation. New paths are sensed and vibrational frequency is increased, causing a rise in consciousness and an opening of new paths. The environment which is experienced is the same, albeit on a higher level. At first, this elevation is temporary but becomes more permanent after embracing the energetic flow of ᚨ Óss (Ansuz). Consciousness touches new possibilities; hints of knowledge experienced during moments of ecstasy. The universal consciousness whispers to it by gently touching it. Realisation of this pushes it to new insights which give rise to new pathways for potential growth.

This is the stage at which ᚱ Reið (Raidho) comes into play, enabling and directing its ascension into these new perceived heights. Now is the time for it to focus down a specific path to realisation. Consciousness has a purpose guided by the energies of ᚱ Reið (Raidho).

It is important to note that the path itself is not yet revealed as being the right one at this stage, hence confusion, doubt and uncertainty are still present.

Questioning of whether this was the correct choice is frequently experienced and diversions into other similar paths is common. There is directionality, however, as consciousness knows in WHICH direction it is heading. The intellectual and intuitive aspects of it analyse but there is no knowledge of HOW to reach the destination aimed for. The development it has gained from the previous runic energies have enabled it to be investigative, to delve into the values of experiencing many possibilities until it has found the one suited to the task at hand (and its Self). This initiates the move from ᚱ Reið (Raidho) to ᚲ Kaun (Kenaz).

Upon reaching the ᚲ Kaun (Kenaz) state, something wonderful happens. The result of all the experiencing, battling and testing of various paths comes to a gradual end. The flames of ᚲ Kaun (Kenaz) illuminate and show consciousness where it is and what it has been doing. Suddenly, it finds that it has been the navigator all along and that its own powers propel it forward into a direction which is perfectly suited to expression of the uniqueness of its being. No longer is it dabbling in the dark and desperately trying to find its way. It can now use the light within to guide itself. Environmental and external experiential needs start to dull down and it goes through another important inner focal period where it comes to realise that it is complete and has the knowledge within itself to sustain its purpose without having to rely on outward signs and directions. At this point, its path is set and chosen with the full insight of conscious realisation, unlike in the ᚠ Óss (Ansuz) state where the state of ecstasy automatically lifts you onto a new without conscious input.

Having reached the inner light of consciousness,

it has gained self-realisation and knowledge of its path forward. The only two things which remain for it to achieve are the X Gjöf (Gebo) and ᚹ Vin (Wunjo) states. As it progresses further along its chosen path, it comes across other forms of consciousness and begins to look elsewhere outside of its Self or its immediate environment.

This signals the entry into X Gjöf (Gebo)'s influence, giving rise to the need to experience other conscious beings in order to know what other forms and types of conscious expression there are. The pull towards others starts to gain momentum as does the need to unite, as now power and knowledge, experience and wisdom are sought through others. In these unions, consciousness learns about how its own Self is reflected through the not-Self and learns to see things from the perceptions of others and experience reality it is currently in as reflected by other manifestations of consciousness. This ranges from the need to unite with other human beings, the need to have pets, the need to cherish nature and so forth. It is a fundamental need for reflected and 'non-self-sourced' experience.

Let us keep in mind that these exchanges offered by the energies of X Gjöf (Gebo), are not always positive. We all know too well of relationships which turn sour, horrific events which can befall one during this intimate interaction and so forth. However, the X Gjöf (Gebo) influences are there to teach us that even those negative experiences are just as valuable. They too push consciousness onwards into new heights through the resolution of conflicts. Without those we would be in states of perfect contentment. These eventually lead to stasis.

As long as consciousness does not fall into stasis, this will then signal the start of ᛈ Vin (Wunjo)'s influence. This last rune in the first Ætt teaches the laws of harmonic and disharmonic being, where even two contradictory poles can be in harmony with each other, or two identical poles can conflict to no end. ᛈ Vin (Wunjo) brings consciousness into a state which can no longer be set off course by chaos. The harmonic influences it has on consciousness can be so profound that one simply cannot be shaken no matter what happens. It is an initial glimpse into a perfect state. At this point, ᛈ Vin (Wunjo) brings the power of choice often hinted at by the wish-fulfilling aspects of the rune, for to make a wish is to also make a choice with willed acceptance and acknowledgement. When you seek fulfilment of a given wish, you are choosing for that event, path or possibility to be open to you and for you to follow it no matter what! Here, consciousness has started directing its own path and choosing how it will reach it. When one is dealing with physical events, more often than not the choices will involve life on the physical level of Midgard, such as family, job, health and so forth. When dealing with the final ascent, the choices made will often involve the spiritual or dimensional domain.

In any case, ᛈ Vin (Wunjo) presents a critically important opportunity for anyone working through this state of conscious growth. It is that of choice. At this stage, one can choose to turn back and inverse one's growth to move forward to the next stage or not choose at all. This last option however would leave one within the ᛈ Vin (Wunjo) energy permanently, leading to evolutionary stasis.

THE SECOND ÆTT

Having made choices and gained further experience from living through them, consciousness realises that it has too spread itself too thin outwards. Gradually, it loses its original focus or loses sight of its own nature or path until the influences of H Hagall (Hagalaz) start to make themselves felt. These then 'purify' the conscious Self, forcing it to work through what is holding it back. Burning through the mesh of burdens it has gained and reaffirming its nature and desires gives it the fuel to move on until finally the ↑ Nauð (Nauthiz) fires start to arise. Having regained the purity of desire and directionality, the fires of need propel that movement forward once more.

As desire is re-awoken, the influences of I Íss (Isa) allow them to consolidate, synchronizing the Self and solidifying the drive towards them which provides the foundations upon which they can be built. The end result of this is a new seed sown by consciousness itself within consciousness. This seed represents all that it desires, the motivations behind it and the direction in which it seeks to move. New matter is acquired during the I Íss (Isa) stage, in raw solid state, to serve as the fuel for the fires of ↑ Nauð (Nauthiz) to consume and provide kinetic movement of consciousness.

Once it crystalizes, the influences of ✦ Ár (Jera) come into play. As ✦ Ár (Jera) turns slowly and surely, the seed drives conscious to experience that which was seeded within. The powers of ✦ Ár (Jera) will keep cycling until those experiences and desires gain sufficient momentum to either be lived through or manifested. Consciousness will have gained the drive to push forward and realise what it has seeded.

Once life seems to have nothing else to offer, the move into ᛈ Perð (Pertho)'s energy takes place. One can regress at this point if depression, drugs and other forms of escapism take root. This is the challenge of ᛈ Perð (Pertho), the rune of the void. It is only by reinventing itself that consciousness is able to move out of the deep dark waters of ᛈ Perð (Pertho), and it is only by realising the divinity within or setting its gaze upon the divine that it enters the realm of ᛇ Jór (Eihwaz).

Having reached this phase, ᛇ Jór (Eihwaz) is encountered and unleashed. It drags consciousness throughout all the worlds in order to experience that which the seed produced during its seeding. Only once all those experiences have been lived through and assimilated does the ᛇ Jór (Eihwaz) stage of growth complete. Disillusionment or boredom of experiencing signals the end of this stage of consciousness development. Nothing piques the interest, nothing excites, nothing seems to capture the spark of desire.

The move from ᛇ Jór (Eihwaz) towards ᛉ Ýr (Elhaz) is one of the longest and most tedious of all. ᛉ Ýr (Elhaz) initiates a rise upwards, a type of spiralling of consciousness beyond the limits of the purely physical and into the realisation that there is something more to life than purely the material aspects of reality. ᛉ Ýr (Elhaz) then propels things upwards. It raises the vibrations and scope of consciousness, forcing an evolutionary jump. Divinity stirs, the Self expands and new concepts, possibilities and dimensions are opened to it. This gives rise to the influence of ᛋ Sól (Sowilo).

With the onset of ⚡ Sól (Sowilo)'s power, the Will is synthesized. Consciousness has new vision as established by ᛦ Ýr (Elhaz) and it is the power of ⚡ Sól (Sowilo) which now pushes it forward, strengthening it and giving it the energetic drive to push forward towards the challenges of the third Ætt. The effects of ⚡ Sól (Sowilo) pull more of the Spark of Self into the domain of consciousness. It becomes more and more in-tune with the realisations of the Self and as the light of ⚡ Sól (Sowilo) does this, it pulses that Self out into the realities in which it is functioning, living or experiencing.

THE THIRD ÆTT

Having arrived at the third Ætt, the Self is presented with the challenges of spiritual confrontation. It is only with the influence of ↑ Týr (Tiwaz) that it can strive forward. Having awoken to the realisation of the divine dimension of reality (via ᛦ Ýr (Elhaz)) and gained the drive to move forward by Will and Self expression (via ⚡ Sól (Sowilo)), it enters the final stage of confrontations on the spiritual level of reality. It is here that the powers of ↑ Týr (Tiwaz) start to shine. With its help, consciousness can overcome those positive or negative forces which seek to hold it back and, in doing so, gains additional strengths. It realises that it has to become something more than it was previously. This battle is a fight for what it sees as its own just and rightful path; it fights for its own Self. It no longer echoes outwards 'I AM' but now has moved onto 'I AM THAT WHICH I AM', issuing this as both a challenge and a statement of Self-expression and realisation.

Having battled its way through the challenges of ↑ Týr (Tiwaz), ᛒ Bjarkan (Berkano) signals a spiritual gathering of resources. This is a foetal phase in which consciousness goes through a type of re-birthing and integration of experiences, victories and new directionality in which it is determined to grow. Unlike the ᚱ Reið (Raidho) directionality setting, this one is not only more vast in scope but is also there to capture the experiential growth, self-realisations and expression of the essence of Self. The ᛒ Bjarkan (Berkano) energies provide nourishing and growth matter needed for it to take the next step up the developmental pathway. Having achieved sufficient expansion, the energies of ᛖ Eykur (Ehwaz) start to act upon it, signalling the end of the incubation period of ᛒ Bjarkan (Berkano) and the emergence of an enhanced fully functional spiritual consciousness.

As it emerges from the ᛒ Bjarkan (Berkano) stage, the first challenge for the new Self is to acknowledge as well as learn and mastery its supporting eco-systems. This is the purpose of ᛖ Eykur (Ehwaz), which pushes the Self through learning of its actual components and structures. This stage can last as long as it needs to. Only upon gaining mastery and awareness of all its aspects will the powers of ᛗ Maður (Mannaz) start to make their impressions upon it.

ᛗ Maður (Mannaz) takes this development a stage further. Whereas ᛖ Eykur (Ehwaz) required gaining knowledge and mastery over the individual aspects, ᛗ Maður (Mannaz) initiates the other side of the coin, forcing consciousness to integrate functionally and realise its new Self as a whole rather than individual parts. ᛗ Maður (Mannaz) signals a unification unlike any other, as consciousness manifested in all ways and forms. These are now all re-integrated within a cohesive singular being embedded by consciousness. Once this is realised, it forces a move from ᛗ Maður (Mannaz) into ᛚ Lögur (Laguz), at which point the fully realised and integrated spiritual Self starts to tap into the universal flows of life in order to initiate the shaping of realities according to its Will.

ᛚ Lögur (Laguz) provides the Self with not only the substance out of which these realities can be shaped but also with a direct access into the conscious not subject to inner awareness. The two functions reflect off each other, hence the unperceived parts of reality. The fluid energetic flows prompt the shaping of new realities into which the energies of ᛚ Lögur (Laguz) flow and manifest. These are then used as a reflective experiential mechanism for the new Self to learn about unperceived parts of itself which gave rise to this manifestation. This in turn leads to the next input for reality shaping. This wave of prompting via manifestation and reflection back to the conscious for assimilation goes on and on until a synchronisation of all levels of conscious awareness occurs. This synchronisation signals the first glimmer of influence from ◇ Ing (Ingwaz). As that influence grows, a new seeding stage is entered. Unlike the seeding of ᛒ Bjarkan (Berkano), this one is not based on growth from external factors. The ◇ Ing (Ingwaz) seeding signals a merging of the functions of conscious awareness. It is an entirely internal process which uses reality as a reflection mechanism.

The onset of ᛗ Dagur (Dagaz) signals the end of the ◇ Ing (Ingwaz) process. Moving out of ◇ Ing (Ingwaz), consciousness reaches the light of ᛗ Dagur (Dagaz) and enters a state of enlightenment. It has become fully integrated internally and externally, having mastered the lessons of the physical side of existence in the first Ætt, the cosmic side of things in the second and has gained mastery of its very Self in the third.

ᛗ Dagur (Dagaz) and ᛟ Óðal (Othala) function side by side. ᛗ Dagur (Dagaz) gives rise to enlightenment of consciousness and ᛟ Óðal (Othala) serves to ground it into this new foundation. The ᛟ Óðal (Othala) influences serve to establish an additional layer on the very core of what the Self was, is and is meant to be. In order to enable consciousness to do so, it will have to investigate and experience the previous layers of its own being, those which made it what it is at this stage in its evolution. This is the great work of ᛟ Óðal (Othala). It is only once this learning and experiencing reaches the end that new layers can be added to the foundations of ᛟ Óðal (Othala).

The first pass through this runic field of influence is the hardest, as it entails dealing with all of one's own past and inherited ancestral influences. Doing this enables the Self to gain from them and grow. Once complete, a second aspect of ᛟ Óðal (Othala) unfolds which enables the entire Self to build upon itself, establishing a new set of dimensions. The Self is no longer just the physical that it started off as during the initial phase of ᚠ Fé (Fehu). It now has the opportunity to integrate its spiritual awakening with the physical, thus becoming a spiritual Self within the physical.

Completing this ascension causes it to face the three Ætt in reverse order. They are now descended from ᛟ Óðal (Othala) back to ᚠ Fé (Fehu) as the spiritual Self seeks to gain mastery of the physical aspects of its beings. This time, however, the focus is on forcing the spiritual self onto the physical state of being.

The physical then becomes divine and the divine gains physicality. Consciousness turns outwards from within in order to learn of existence, and then this inverses to the state where its focus is from the outside of itself inwards. All these layers of growth happen at the same time, ending in the final state where a fully integrated Self and consciousness starts its final path up from ᚠ Fé (Fehu) one last time towards ᛟ Óðal (Othala).

Discussions of the final pass through the runic fields will be left till a later time for now due to a number of reasons. The primary reason is that this final ascent is far from linear, unlike the first two. During the third pass, the Self does not start at ᚠ Fé (Fehu) and work up to ᛟ Óðal (Othala) from rune to rune as it did previously. Rather, it finds itself at a given runic state and works from there by tapping into any other rune in a random order. It is akin to standing at a given rune and jumping from rune to rune as needed before returning to the first. One then simply moves to 'stand' on another rune and does jumping phase again.

The order in which the move from rune to rune, the order in which one jumps from that base and which directions the jumps are made is what determines the end result of what you will become. The amount of time the Self is exposed to each rune's power will have a significant impact on the end results. It is designed to produce totally unique spirituo-phyiscal beings unlike any other. It is impossible to replicate the process just as it is impossible to produce two totally same beings.

This should provide you with good insight into the evolution of consciousness through the runic currents and powers. We will look at their practical use along with more detailed information on each of them at a later time. For the time being, gaining a general feel of the rune's functions on consciousness itself is all that is required.

Advanced: Runic Trance & Consciousness

This was originally meant to be one of the advanced topics to be covered in a later publication. Due to its importance, however, the decision was made to include it in the current work and leave the deeper parts of it for a later date (after you have learnt actual High Galdr). We all know that Oðin is a master of runes. He states in the Hávamál that he stains them for the Gods and some for mankind as well.

What we are going to be entering now is shifting from the Oðin dominion into Húnir's as the former ends and the later starts, the borderline between the two Æsir's influences. Up to this point, the focus has been on Oðin's side of this balance but from now on we will step into Húnir's with a firm stance.

Two main things are being explored in these two practices. The first is initiating trance states using runic energy. In other words, we are going to send the mind-reason (Hugr) and physical body (Lik) into deep trance states by using them and the spirit (Óðr) in combination with specific rune currents. The second thing on which we are going to start focussing is elevating the consciousness and awareness to new levels of function via those runic currents.

A few words of warning here when practicing these methods: always make sure to remove the rune's energy from whichever part of your Self you call it forth into unless otherwise expressly stated in the instructions! Otherwise, it will constantly exert influence over you in ways you might not even be aware. Runes are not things to be left active willy-nilly around the place. Leaving a rune energy or rune stream flowing will wreak havoc on your internal dynamics of the Self, which you need to maintain balanced for the full awaking and unification of the Self. Additionally, by leaving those currents active you run the risk of them going astray and losing control over them. A rune master without control is no rune master at all.

Prerequisites: since this material was intended for a later book, it taps into knowledge which you will be expected to have but might not yet possess. Most of those requirements revolve around the runes themselves which we will pad out in here. However, there is a need to understand how the nervous system flows out from the spine in the human body. You did not think that you could master the Self without an understanding of the body now, did you? All you need to do is look up the spine and the nervous system either in a book or online. There is no need for knowledge on how they work or their medical applications but you do need to be able to locate and feel your own spine and the nerves flowing from it.

Ensure that you are comfortable setting the Hugr Raven to flight and able to shift into the spirit (Óðr). You must have mastered the first stage of intent as outlined in this publication as well.

Having covered all the pre-requisites time to have some fun! Runic work is best done with a playful childish mind-set combined with the seriousness of an adult. What we will be learning to do at this stage is to not only set the Hugr Raven to flight but also to unite with it fully. In other words, you will become one with your own Hugr. This type of unity opens up parts of the higher functions of the human mind. We are going to take things one step further than what Oðin does in the Eddas. He sends out his Hugr and Minni to observe things and whisper back what they have seen. That is his way of bringing those higher parts of mental function within the reach of his conscious awareness. In some ways, the limitations of the human mind make this advanced method easier for us to access than would be the case for a much more potent mind such as Oðin's. Fasten your spiritual seatbelts, ladies and gents! It is time to take off.

STAGE 1: ESTABLISHING ÓÐRERIR INNER BOUNDARIES

The process for doing this is quite simple. To start, relax and allow the world to fade out of your awareness. Make sure you are comfortable to avoid being disturbed by your body. Begin becoming aware of the Óðr (see 'The Spirit of Húnir Awakens (Part 1)' – Becoming Aware of the Óðr). Shift into it as much as possible and intend yourself to remain rooted there for the duration of this practice. The next step involves shifting into the brain regions for the Hugr and executing the 'Setting the Hugr Raven to flight' while preserving awareness of the Óðr at the same time! Takes a little practice but you will find it easy enough once it clicks into place. When your awareness has been shifted successfully into the Hugr, take flight and turn around to face your actual physical body (Lik). You want to position yourself at the level of your solar plexus (point of the midriff). Push forward, letting the Hugr Raven's beak dive into your flesh, piercing it. Keep pushing in until you enter the physical completely. Upon entering the physical, focus on diving deeper and deeper until you reach the spirit (Óðr) deep within.

Knowing when you have reached the spirit (Óðr) is the trickiest part for most when they first attempt this. Upon entry, you will see a vast darkness which is actually a type of very subtle energy which only appears dark because there is no source of illumination for it. It looks a lot like the vast empty space you used in previous practices when focussing on the inside of your body. Spend a few moments to readjust your sight and you will be able to perceive it as a translucent whiteness (for most people) ranging to a brilliant whiteness (for highly advanced individuals and rune masters). Other subtle variations in sub-hues are normal and are indicators of individualistic characteristics of our own spirit (Óðr). There is no such thing as a 'dark' or 'black' spirit. That would be a manifestation of the Gap. Spirit (Óðr) always manifests as a light even in what is often misunderstood as 'dark spirits'. On the energetic level of reality, things are somewhat different but at this level of abstraction, it is either white, a translucent-white, light or does not exist. If this knowledge bothers your sensibilities, too bad — you will have to live with it.

Hugr Merging into Óðrerir Formation
(From Hugr projection you fly into your own body)

Those little quirks aside, once you see, feel or hear the energy of your spirit (Óðr), dive into it. Once the Hugr Raven is swimming in the midst of spirit (Óðr), intend it to expand and reshape. Expand its shape until it is an exact replica of your physical form (Lik). What you will end up with is a shape that looks like your body (Lik) with the bluish glow of the Hugr Raven and filled with your spirit (Óðr) pulsing through and within it. Allow this to expand out. You will notice after a few moments of expansion that it is expanding from deep within the physical outwards. Allow it to keep expanding until its size is slightly larger than your physical. You want it about ½ inch to 1-inch maximum outside of the physical. In other words, it contains the physical form within itself but just barely.

If you have been paying close attention during this entire process, you will notice that you are in a very deep trance by this point in your practice. For some, this might even be one of the deepest levels they have ever reached. Spiritually and energetically, you have merged the active manifestation of your 'mind' (Hugr) with the spirit (Óðr), given it boundaries from which you can consciously control it or function within (shaping) and then expanded it all beyond but including the physical (Lik). In effect, what you are learning to do is to bridge the mental and spirit with the physical. You are within yourself, forcing the spiritual to manifest in matter and partially uplift the material to a higher level of functioning, dragging all the spirit (Óðr) energies into manifestation and empowering it. Your senses and perceptions will have shifted to a greater extent. Do not analyse it; just experience it. You can dissect the experience as much as you like once you are done. Get used to getting to this point as much as possible.

There are no special closing steps or processes for this practice. Here all we do is leave the Hugr as it is without splitting it up. All you need to do is return to your normal awareness and leave it as is. This is just stage 1 of the practice. Once comfortable with it, it is time to proceed.

Quick Steps

1. Relax and allow the world to fade from awareness
2. Become aware of the spirit (Óðr) and shift your awareness into it as much as possible whilst intending it to remain rooted there.
3. From there, do the Setting the Hugr Raven to flight practice and split your awareness across both (the spirit (Óðr) and mind (Hugr)).
4. From the Hugr Raven, take flight and face your physical body (Lik).
5. Position yourself in the Raven so that you are facing the solar plexus of your physical form.
6. Dive into the flesh, piercing through into it. Once in the physical, keep piercing inwards through the energy body (Hamr) and then into the spirit (Óðr) itself.
7. When you perceive the vast empty space within filled with subtle energy, you will notice the brilliance of your spirit (Óðr) with what-ever appropriate sub-hues to the whites it may have.

8. Experience the energy of your spirit (Óðr) as an outside observer.

9. Fly into it and merge into its quasi-form (which will look like your physical but only in terms of shape and even that will be loose rather than dense).

10. Allow the Hugr Raven to spill into it as you previously did in other practices but this time, it is spilling into the spirit (Óðr) itself and merging with its energy and adopting its shape. It will expand outwards as if radiating out. As it does, it will radiate thought the energy body (Hamr) into and through the physical up to 1 inch or so around the body.

11. Get used to this new perceptive reach. Enjoy it, observe it, take note of it.

12. Note that we are not 'de-coupling' the mind (Hugr) and the spirit (Óðr) here. Simply leave this to remain and gradually return to your normal awareness.

What we are going to be achieving here is one of the greatest mysteries accessible to a human mind — something sought throughout the ages. We are, in effect, gaining practical use of the Norse equivalent to the 'Holy Grail'.

ÓÐRERIR: THE NORSE 'HOLY GRAIL'

So much has been taken from the Norse tradition and incorporated into others it would not be surprising to find that the holy grail of Arthurian legends and the 'holy chalice' of Christianity were actually sourced from within the Hávamál. It is a collection of Norse traditional poems found in the The Poetic Edda, 13th century as a compilation of long established oral traditions of the Indo-European people. Bellows (1936) states that the components forming the Hávamál date to "a very early time"[33], some sources go as far as drawing from linguistic similarities to trace some of its contents as far back as the 1st century, others even further back in time. Irrespective of timeline, what interests us is its teachings.

In the Hávamál, we have the concept of the Óðrerir, which is defined both as the mead of poetry and the vessel which contains it depending on which occurrence of the term we look at. As usual, scholars argue about definitions and linguistics, in this case both definitions are correct. Let us take a quick detour and look at its occurrences in a little more detail. In the Thorpe translation[34] we have:

> Of a well-assumed form
> I made good use:
> few things fail the wise;
> for Odhrærir
> is now come up
> to men's earthly dwellings (stanza 107)

and

> Potent songs nine
> from the famed son I learned
> of Bölthorn, Bestla's sire,
> and a draught obtained
> of the precious mead,
> drawn from Odhrærir. (stanza 142)

From the W. H. Auden and P. B. Taylor translation we get:

> Nine lays of power
> I learned from the famous Bolthor, Bestla' s father:
> He poured me a draught of precious mead,
> Mixed with magic Óðrerir[35].

Óðrerir is also mentioned in the Myth of Kvasir (Skáldskaparmál 5 in Prose Edda) with reference to the Mead of Poetry. Where Kvasir's blood was contained in two vats and a pot called Boðn, Són and Óðrerir respectively.

In the first quote (stanza 107), we get our first indication of this important concept. It starts off by mentioning a well-assumed form, which hints at the shaping of spirit (Óðr) and, as we will see later on, the shadow (Sal) and energy body (Hamr). Once you have form, you gain a certain scope of action or potential ability which Oðin admon-ishes us to make good of and hints at how such things do not fail the wise. The next part which discusses how Óðrerir has come up to the dwelling of men points to this mystical container becoming available to mankind. It 'comes up' because it is only fully formed once you have formed it on all levels of the Self. In order to do so, the energetic level is formed from feet upwards. We will go into a lot more detail about this entire process when looking at that level of reality and Self. For now, this should be sufficient in order understand to what the stanza is referring to. Remember these are all pointers to know-ledge. The fascinating concept is that of the shaping (well-assumed form) and the container (Óðrerir). Both are indicative of containment of something. **Form gives expression to purpose and function.** This point is made painfully clear in stanza 142 when Oðin mentions the precious mead which is drawn from Óðrerir.

When it comes to the Mead of Poetry, we know from the Sagas that it provides one with inspiration, makes one wise and a poet or scholar[37]. In other words, it is an elixir of the mind. We get a fascinating insight into this from the W. H. Auden and P. B. Taylor trans-lation where it states that "He poured me a draught of precious mead, mixed with magic Óðrerir". 'He' in this case is an indication of the giant. There are numerous forms of mead throughout the Eddas and Sagas. The mead of poetry and inspiration is from the Myth of Kvasir, the precious substance obtained during Oðin's sacrificial trial and bestows knowledge, power and spiritual insights obtained from the domain of the giants in Gunnlöð. Do note that Snorri's account in the Myth of Kyasir differs to the earlier one found in the Hávamál. In the latter, the giantess had the mead and this did not involve the creation and killing of Kyasir at all. Additionally, this was not only a Mead of Inspiration but of power and growth as well. Then we have the Mead of Memory found in the Hyndluljóð (from the Poetic Eddas) that was gifted to Óttarr by Freya to prevent him from falling into the slumber of death (instead he arises in Vallhala).

We will see how formation of the Mead of Memory is used to prevent the endless slumber of death and descent into Niflheim from overcoming the completed Self, how the Mead of Power (and initiation) enables activations of the runes, and how the Mead of Inspiration (mind) enables awakening of awareness to other realities and enhances perceptions. A further reference to the Óðrerir is found in Stanza 2 from Hrafnagaldur Odins (Oðin's Raven Poem):

"The Æsir suspected
an evil scheme,
wights confounded
the weather with magic;
Urður was appointed

Óðhrærir's keeper,
powerful to protect it
from the mightiest winter."[38]

The Raven Poem is a riddle of a poem because it requires an unfolding of the Self to grasp it. Weather typically talks about the mind. The winds, the air and sky ruled by ᚠ Óss (Ansuz) also rule the mind (Óðr, Hugr and Minni combined). The evil scheme is obvious, hence we have discussions of how our minds are clouded from knowledge and disrupted by the working of evil caused by magic cast by the wights. In this same stanza, the second part reveals that the Norn Urð is appointed keeper of the Óðrerir (the above is just an alternative spelling of the word). She is deemed powerful enough to protect it from the 'mightiest winter'. Now in order to understand that, one has look at winter and its icy essence which is stasis. What is being revealed is that Urð, one of the three most powerful beings in Creation, is appointed to keep the Óðrerir from the stasis caused by the evil wights as described in the first part of the stanza, ultimately telling us that our minds and spirits have been confounded by works of evil magic that send the spirit into stasis (or sleep). During this time, Urð, who wove all the fates in Creation, is guarding the Óðrerir. This gives us significant insights into both the link between the Óðrerir and our spirit (Óðr) awakening as well as the importance of it. For the Cosmic Urð to guard it means she will weave the fates in order to ensure it is there when the time comes for it to be rediscovered or needed. This poem gives us the most significant hint as to the importance of this 'cauldron' in which the meads are held.

Let us look at the actual word Óðrerir. We can see it is composed of Óðr and -rerir, and an interesting insight is gained when looking at their definitions. First, we have spirit (Óðr), which as we know is the primary part of the Self on the mental level which we loosely define as Spirit. The second part of the word can be interpreted as a brew, or the action of blending or stirring. In effect, we have the stirring or blending of Spirit into a type of brew. Suddenly, all the different forms of Meads make sense! Depending on what type of spirit you are blending (and what it is blended with), you can produce different types of Mead, which in turn produce different effects.

Lights should be flashing by now in your mind! What if all those lost or detached spirits that we talked about in The Spirit of Húnir Awakens (Part 1) actually serve to produce various meads? What if dead spirits are used to different effects? Could all that not justify the constant formation of new ones? Suddenly the lack of reincarnation makes sense! Incomplete Selves are taken as nourishment for complete ones in order to ensure the continuation of growth of the cosmos and Yggdrasil. We are not concerned with such things at this point in time, however, as that is the domain of the Gods and Goddesses. For our purposes, we are concerned with the formation of our own Óðrerir, which is exactly what we are doing. The awakening of your spirit (Óðr) is the first step into forming it into a fully functional Óðrerir (or 'holy grail' which was always within each and every one of us! No wonder no-one has found it to date....).

In these practices, we are taking the first step in its formation. When we look at the energy body (Hamr) and shadow (Sal), we will be taking the final two steps. By learning to access the actual Galdr, we will then be able to fill our Óðrerir and mix in our Spirit (Óðr) with various rune streams of power which, when drank by our energy body (Hamr), will produce wonders non-rune masters cannot even imagine.

ᛋ Entering into Runic Trance: Strengthening Óðrerir Inner Boundaries

Having learnt how to establish the inner boundaries of the Óðrerir and using that process to enter into a deeper than usual trance state, it is time to learn how to add the runic layer to the practice. By simply doing this, you will experience a strengthening of the boundaries of your Óðrerir construction. It is important to keep in mind that we are not making an artificial construct of any type. Those typically are used to restrict and control how you can express your Self and should be avoided at all costs, as adding additional structures to your Self is never beneficial no matter how it is presented. There is simply no need for them. All you need is found within you and the runes. This is so much the case that, in our work, we do not even rely on the Gods or Goddesses for any other purpose than knowledge and guidance. You have everything you need — it is simply a matter of learning about it and how to use it. Thus eventually you become a master of your own Self rather than relying on 'gifts', boons, and all sorts of other external tricks which diminish your mastery and develop dependence on another being, which leads to a loss of Self in some way, shape or form.

To begin the trance work, start by establishing the inner boundaries of the Óðrerir. Having established them and hence their shape, maintain awareness of the spirit (Óðr) within and the shape now established by the mind's (Hugr) reshaping. Identify with that shape and feel the spirit (Óðr) pulsating, flowing and radiating within. A minute or two will suffice whilst learning, but with practice you will gain the ability to shift into the required state of mind within an instance at most. Now simply chant one of your selected runes. If you are doing this as part of your High Galdr training, start with ᚠ Fé (Fehu) and work your way through all the runes to ᛟ Óðal (Othala), switching to a new one each time you practice this. Only do one rune at a time and for goodness sake, keep those in the correct order (see Appendix A)! Otherwise, you will overwhelm your spirit (Óðr) and Óðrerir at this point. Growth is gradual and time for adaptation is required. Many fail at properly developing into the most advanced types of skill sets and runic work because they rush and do not allow the Self to assimilate changes, which leaves things incomplete. Avoid doing this and take your time. You need to keep all nine parts of your Self on track. If one feels overwhelmed or left behind, this causes underlying issues which can become very problematic later on. Patience is a virtue!

Chant your rune and feel the space around you fill with its power, its energy and sense its characteristics. Hear the sound of its name and feel its vibrations on the outside boundaries of your newly established Óðrerir. When ready, will (or intend) it to circulate in a anti-clockwise manner around you. Remember to keep the focus on feeling the spiralling energy. As it does, direct this energy to descend to your feet where it will accumulate. Then visualise the shape of the rune in that exact spot as if you were standing on it. During this accumulation, see it mixing with white energy which also naturally pools at your feet up to your ankles and intensify it. When it is done, allow it to explode in two upwards flows, going straight from your feet up the front of the Óðrerir (just visualising it going up the front of the body) and the second stream up the back.

As these flows rise in front and behind you, from within the Óðrerir intend that this energy is pulled into its form. Literally will it to be sucked into it. Since we are working on the mental level of the Self, intent is all that is required to direct things. They respond automatically, providing you have established the intent correctly. The runic energy should be absorbed comp-letely into the Óðrerir and be flooding the spirit (Óðr) (which is within the Óðrerir shape). The final stage is to simply allow this runic energy to remain there. Observe what it does to you, how you feel, what you experience and how you experience it all. This will shift you into the appropriate runic trance. Just go with the flow! If you experience fear, anxiety or resistance, it simply means you need to work more with this rune's trance type. The best thing to do is to reduce the amount of energy you initially pull in through your feet.

When ready to exit this type of trance, you will not be allowing this energy to fade back into Creation. Why? Because you combined it with your own and that would be the equivalent of losing an important part of your own energy which is the exact opposite of what we want. Instead, you are going to intend it to flow into the Hamingja, which by now you should be pretty practiced working with. If not go learn about it BEFORE you do this practice. Leaving the runic energy within your spirit (Óðr) will simply cause massive fluxes which are highly disruptive. The spirit (Óðr) of a human being does not have the innate capacity to hold onto this energy nor to process it. Remember that this is the very first time it will be experiencing this type of direct influence so be nice to your spirit (Óðr)! To drive it all into the Hamingja, focus on the energy that you have been working with (just the one inside of your Óðrerir shape and NOT the universal one) and direct it with intent to flow upwards into the Hamingja on the back. Here, we use the patch on the back not the personalised Hamingja form, unless you are very skilled with the personalised version. You should sense the energy emptying into the Hamingja until there is none left within the Óðrerir form itself. If you observe closely, the only runic energy you will notice is on the inside of the shape of your Óðrerir. It typically looks like a thin layer of fluid energy intermixing with that of the Óðrerir itself. It is the runic current merging with your Óðrerir and strengthening it as well as imbuing it with its prop-erties, which will in turn will amplify the potential of the mind (Hugr) and your spirit (Óðr). This is one of the desired effects so just leave that part of it there.

The final step involves allowing the runic energy around you to fade away. Once you are alone in endless empty space, refocus on your physical body (Lik) and return to your daily awareness. The next time you practice this, move onto the next rune unless you have had any issues or resistances. In that case, repeat the same one for as long as it takes for those issues to fade away.

Quick Steps

1. Start by establishing the inner boundaries of the Óðrerir.
2. Maintain awareness of the spirit (Óðr) and be aware of the boundaries established by the mind (Hugr). Identify with the shape and feel of the spirit (Óðr) pulsating and flowing.
3. Chant (or use High Galdr) a rune you selected to work with from the Runic trance outline. If you are doing your High Galdr training, start with ᚠ Fé (Fehu) and work through each rune in turn. Only do one rune at a time.
4. As the energy of the rune fills the space around you, feel its energy, its power and its essence. Intend and pull the energy around yourself in an anti-clockwise spiralling motion. Feel it strengthening the outer boundaries of the Óðrerir.
5. As it circulates around you, direct it to descend to your feet where it will accumulate and create an energetic pool mixing with brilliant whites. See the shape of the rune

form under your feet.

6. After this pooling, it will concentrate until it finally explodes in an upwards direction on the back and front of your body. It splits into two streams, hence the duality of its upward flow.

7. From within the Óðrerir, intend the flowing energy to be absorbed into it. As soon as you do, it will be 'sucked' into it and integrated into its structure as well as flood the spirit (Óðr) where your awareness has been rooted.

8. Simply allow this energy to stay there and experience it. Observe what it does to you, how it makes you feel and what it does to your mind and perceptions. If it feels over-whelming, just avoid pulling in so much energy from the pool formed at the base of your feet.

9. When you are done enjoying this new state of mind, focus on the energy in your spirit (Óðr) (but leave the energy around your Óðrerir and that absorbed by it) and direct it into your Hamingja.

10. Allow the rest of the energy from the empty space around you to fade. Refocus on your physical body and return to daily awareness.

This is but a glimpse into the more advanced work with runes and rune streams. We will expand on the formation of the Óðrerir in future work until it is fully formed. At that point, you will be able to produce your own and runic types of Meads, as well as have united all the parts of your Self into one single unit which will awaken your Spark of Self to full potential. Drinking the Mead you produce will then unlock further abilities and wonders. You will have your own 'Holy Grail' and it will provide for you whatever it is your Self actually needs.

Trance Types

Depending on what rune energies you use, different trances can be attained. The most commonly described conception of trance among modern metaphysical practitioners is the stasis trance of ᛁ Íss (Isa) which involves silencing the mind, stilling the body and relaxing deeper and deeper into trance. There is nothing wrong with this type of trance and it is exceedingly appropriate for most uses. That should not, however, prevent us from availing ourselves of other types of trance.

From the myths, we gain knowledge of the transformative trances of the Bezerkers of Oðin, travel trances of the Völva and Seidr practitioners and so forth. From the runes we can gain access to all of these and more. There are, in fact, a total of 33 types of runic trances that are directly accessible. For the time being, suffice it to experience the various runic energies during the above given practices until they become second nature and to study the runic influences on evolution of consciousness. Doing those two things will unlock a multitude of insights into these runic trances. When looking at actual High Galdr, we will look into what they are and what each one actually does.

Do not forget to practice working these things out from your own learnings and insights. Doing so is essential to future rune work.

THE ULTIMATE TRANCE
ÓÐR (SPIRIT) PROJECTION

It is now time to learn the final and most important type of projection available to the mental level of the Self — projecting with full awareness in the spirit (Óðr). During this type of projection, both the Hugr and the Minni are automatically carried over as they are part of the spirit (Óðr). What you will experience is being a pure spirit with no restrictions whatsoever. The only difference between you in this state and a random spirit (Óðr) is your anchor in the physical (Lik) or the energy level of the Self. This link will provide feedback and sustenance to you, as well as the ability for anchoring experiences into that level, eventually allowing it to flow up to the archetypal level of the Self.

Sit down and relax. This is the most important part of the practice. Spend a good 5 to 10 minutes letting go of your perceptions of the world, your worries, concerns and so forth. Allowing your body to release as much tension as it naturally can is essential. There is no need to do specific relaxation techniques or to try and force relaxation of each muscle in the body as this only causes additional tension and strain, all of which transfers to the mental level. Just intend to relax and trust your body to do it in the best way for it.

Mentally chant the rune ᛇ Jór (Eihwaz), allowing its deep violet black energy to flood your body. Intend it to push you deeper into trance and facilitate projection of conscious awareness, as well as loosen the bonds of the energy body (Hamr) on the spirit (Óðr).

Once relaxed, spend a few minutes observing your thoughts and achieving as close to inner silence as you can. Next become aware of the spirit (Óðr) and shift your focus into it (see 'The Spirit of Húnir Awakens (Part 1) - Becoming Conscious of the Óðr). Reflect on the fact that it is pure formless energy and hence has no boundaries in either time nor in space. It is the flowing expression of your Self free of all restrictions. Chant the ᚠ Óss (Ansuz) rune and intend for its energy to set you free of the boundaries of flesh and energy body (Hamr).

Bathe in this sense of freedom and lack of boundaries and enjoy it for a few minutes before stepping out of the physical body. Stand to the side of it in your spirit (Óðr). Since it was housed in the physical (Lík) and the inner boundaries of the Óðrerir were formed, the spirit (Óðr) will automatically be the same shape as the physical. Keep it that way for now as we will learn how to shift whilst in the spirit (Óðr) later on. At this moment, simply observe from within the spirit (Óðr), feeling yourself as the spirit (Óðr) and only the spirit (Óðr).

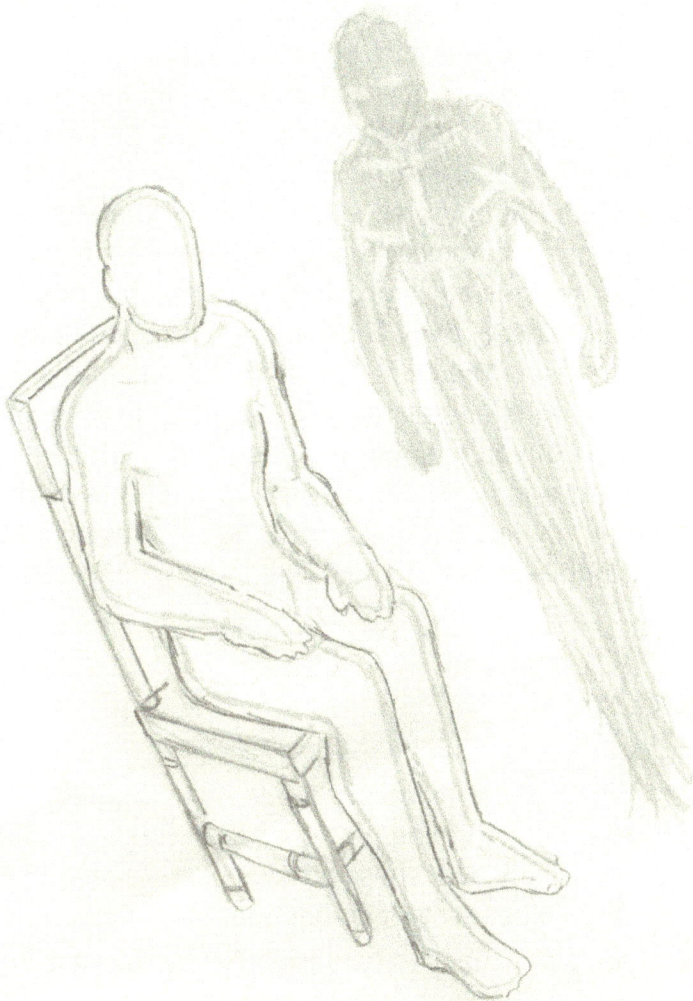

Óðr (Spirit) Projection
(Standing in the Óðr next to your own body and Hamr)

Nothing else matters; nothing else is relevant other than you being the spirit (Óðr). As soon as you have a firm footing inside of it, mentally use the ᛟ Óðal (Othala) rune. This will make it your current 'home' setting and ground you inside of it. It will also solidify perceptive abilities in it. Next, look at your physical body resting in whatever position you left it in trance and think about how it is just a body — it is no longer YOU. What we are trying to achieve is a temporary disassociation from the physical (Lik). Be careful that you are NOT rejecting it! You are simply disassociating from it. When done, step back into it by intending to remerge within the energy body and the physical. Spend a few moments using the ᛗ Maður (Mannaz) rune, allowing its free-flowing airy red energy to flood you, each and every part of you harmonising and at ease with every other part and focus on relinking to the parts of the Self that you left a few moments ago. Focus on how you are now inside of them and they are YOU once more.

Quick Steps

1. Spend a few minutes relaxing. Focus on relaxing, allowing the world to fade from your immediate awareness but do not force relaxation. Just allow it to happen.

2. Mentally chant (or use High Galdr) the rune ᛇ Jór (Eihwaz) see its deep violet energy flood your body whilst intending it to push you into deeper trance, enable projection of conscious awareness and loosen the bonds in between the energy body (Hamr) and the spirit (Óðr).

3. Once relaxed enter into inner silence as best as you can.

4. Shift your focus into the spirit (Óðr) (see 'Becoming Conscious of the Óðr' in The Spirit of Húnir Awakens (Part 1)).

5. Reflect on the part of you which is pure energy, formless, with no boundaries, restrictions or limitations to time or space.

6. Chant the rune ᚠ Óss (Ansuz) and intend its energy to set you free of the boundaries imposed upon you by your physical body (Lik) and your energy body (Hamr). Bathe in this sense of freedom.

7. Having established this overriding perception of freedom, from within your spirit (Óðr) focus on stepping out of the physical (Lik) and energetic bodies (Hamr and Sal).

8. As you do, you will be in exactly the same shape as your physical has.

9. Meditate on the fact that you are now in your spirit (Óðr) shaped as your physical body (Lik).

10. Use ᛟ Óðal (Othala) from within the spirit (Óðr), unleashing its energies within the spirit (Óðr) as it stands next to but is separate from your physical body.

11. Observe the body. Feel the separateness from it but ensure you do not reject it as this will cause disharmony in the Self.

12. When done, intend to remerge with the physical and step into it.

13. When your awareness is back in the physical body (Lik). Use the ᛗ Maður (Mannaz) rune, allowing its free-flowing airy red energy to

flood you, each and every part of you harmonising and at ease with every other part.

14. Return to normal awareness and have a cup of coffee, tea, or a bite to eat to ground your Self.

This, ladies and gents, completes our initial work with the Óðr, Hugr and Minni. It also sets the foundation work for Óðrerir and intent mastery, whose importance cannot be overemphasised. May the Spirit of Húnir smile upon you and guide you in your efforts with this work.

Frank A. Rúnaldrar

APPENDIXES

APPENDIX A

Table of Runic Name Alternatives

Rune	Numeric Value	Icelandic Name	Germanic Name
ᚠ	1	Fé	Fehu
ᚢ	2	Úr	Uruz
ᚦ	3	Þurs	Thurisaz
ᚨ	4	Óss (Ás)	Ansuz
ᚱ	5	Reið	Raidho
ᚲ	6	Kaun	Kenaz
ᚷ	7	Gjöf	Gebo
ᚹ	8	Vin	Wunjo
ᚺ	9	Hagall	Hagalaz
ᚾ	10	Nauð	Nauthiz
ᛁ	11	Íss	Isa
ᛃ	12	Ár	Jera
ᛈ	13	Perð	Pertho
ᛇ	14	Jór	Eihwaz
ᛉ	15	Ýr	Elhaz
ᛋ	16	Sól	Sowilo
ᛏ	17	Týr	Tiwaz
ᛒ	18	Bjarkan	Berkano
ᛖ	19	Eykur	Ehwaz
ᛗ	20	Maður	Mannaz
ᛚ	21	Lögur	Laguz
ᛝ	22	Ing	Ingwaz
ᛞ	23	Dagur	Dagaz
ᛟ	24	Óðal	Othala

APPENDIX B

References

1. Rúnaldrar, F. A. (2016). "The 'Breath of Oðin' Awakens - Secrets of the Önd, Hamingja & 'Norse Luck' Unveiled". London: Bastian & West. ISBN: 978-0-9955343-0-8

2. ante

3. Constance, I. (1980). Strange Footprints on the Land, Harper & Row, ISBN 0-06-022772-9

4. Sturluson, S. (1964). The Prose Edda: Tales from Norse Mythology, translated Young, J. I., California Press.

5. Rúnaldrar, F. A. (2017). "The Spirit of Húnir Awakens (Part 1)", London, Bastian & West ISBN: 978-0-9955343-2-2, p.70

6. Rúnaldrar, F. A. (2016). "The Breath of Oðin Awakens – Secrets of the Önd, Hamingja & 'Norse Luck' Unveiled", London, Bastian & West. ISBN: 978-0-9955343-0-8

7. Rúnaldrar, F. A. (2017). "The Spirit of Húnir Awakens (Part 1)", London, Bastian & West ISBN: 978-0-9955343-2-2, p.153

8. Rúnaldrar, F. A. (2016). "The Breath of Oðin Awakens
– Secrets of the Önd, Hamingja & 'Norse Luck' Unveiled",
London, Bastian & West. ISBN: 978-0-9955343-0-8,
p. 24

9. Travis, J. A., Craddock, J. A., Tuszynski, S. H. (2012).
"Cytoskeletal Signaling: Is Memory Encoded in Micro-
tubule Lattices" by CaMKII Phosphorylation? PLoS
Computational Biology, 8 (3): e1002421 DOI: 10.1371/
journal.pcbi.1002421

10. Rúnaldrar, F. A. (2017). "The Spirit of Húnir Awakens
(Part 1)", London, Bastian & West ISBN: 978-0-9955343-
2-2, p.109

11. Reimann, M. W., Nolte, M., Scolamiero, M., et al.
(2017). "Cliques of Neurons Bound into Cavities Provide
a Missing Link between Structure and Function". Frontiers
in Computational Neuroscience, 11 DOI: 10.3389/fncom.
2017.00048

12. Frontiers. (2017). "'Multi-dimensional universe' in
brain networks: Using mathematics in a novel way in
neuroscience, scientists demonstrate that the brain
operates on many dimensions, not just the 3 dimensions
that we are accustomed to." ScienceDaily. Retrieved
June 18, retrieved from www.sciencedaily.com/releases
/2017/06/170612094100.htm

13. Church, G. M., Gao, Y., Kosuri, S. (2012). 'Next-
Generation Digital Information Storage in DNA', Science,
Aug ed. Doi: 10.1126/science.1226355

14. Anthony, S. (2012). 'Biological computer can decrypt images stored in DNA', ExtremeTech (online edition), February, retrieved from: http://www.extremetech.com/extreme/117463-biological-computer-can-decrypt-images-stored-in-dna

15. Extance, A. (2016). 'How DNA could store all the world's data', Nature 537, 22–24 (01 September) doi: 10.1038/537022a

16. Dias, B. G., Ressler, K. J. (2014), 'Parental olfactory experience influences behavior and neural structure in subsequent generations', Nature Neuroscience Vol 17 No 1 – Jan 2014 Ed. doi:10.1038/nn.3594

17. For further reading on these topics look at the research by Dr Vanessa LoBue, Rutgers University (https://www.childstudycenter-rutgers.com)

18. Hackett, J. A., Sengupta, R., Zylicz, J. J., et al. (2013). 'Germline DNA Demethylation Dynamics and Imprint Erasure Through 5-Hydroxymethylcytosine', Science, 25 Jan, Vol. 339, Issue 6118, pp. 448-452, DOI: 10.1126/science.1229277

19. Y. Hara, F. Yuk, R. Puri, W. G. M. Janssen, P. R. Rapp, J. H. Morrison (2013). "Presynaptic mitochondrial morphology in monkey prefrontal cortex correlates with working memory and is improved with estrogen treatment". Proceedings of the National Academy of Sciences, 2013; DOI: 10.1073/pnas.1311310110

20. Thorpe, B., (Trans) (1907) in Edda Sæmundar Hinns Frôða The Edda of Sæmund the Learned. Part I. London Trübner & Co, p 21.

21. Sturluson, S. (1179-1241). Heimskringla , retrieved from: https://www.wisdomlib.org/scandinavia/book/heimskringla

22. Krists minni, Michaêls minni, etc. (Source: Grimm, J. (1835). Deutsche Mythologie (1835), chapter 3)

23. Grimm, J. (1882). Teutonic mythology. Stallybrass, J. S. (tr.), George Bell and Sons. Dover Publications (1966, 2004) – reprint

24. Sturluson, S. (1179-1241). Heimskringla , retrieved from: https://www.wisdomlib.org/scandinavia/book/heimskringla

25. Rúnaldrar, F. A. (2016). "The Breath of Oðin Awakens – Secrets of the Önd, Hamingja & 'Norse Luck' Unveiled", London, Bastian & West. ISBN: 978-0-9955343-0-8, p.33-36

26. ante p.1

27. ante

28. Ramirez, S., Liu, X., Lin, P. A., Suh, J. et al (2013). Creating a False Memory in the Hippocampus. Science, 26 July, 387-391 DOI: 10.1126/science.1239073

29. Schacter, D. L., Addis, D. R., Hassabis, D., Martin, V. C., Spreng, R. N., & Szpunar, K. K. (2012). The Future of Memory: Remembering, Imagining, and the Brain. Neuron, 76(4), 10.1016/j.neuron.2012.11.001. http://doi.org/10.1016/j.neuron.2012.11.001

30. Ehinger, B. V., Häusser, K., Ossandón, J. P., König, P., (2017). Humans treat unreliable filled-in percepts as more real than veridical ones. eLife, 6 DOI: 10.7554/eLife.21761

31. Institute for Quality and Efficiency in Health Care (2016), "How does our sense of taste work?", Informed Health Online, retrieved from: https://www.ncbi.nlm.nih.gov/pubmedhealth/PMH0072592/

32. Rúnaldrar, F. A. (2017). "The Spirit of Húnir Awakens (Part 1)", London, Bastian & West ISBN: 978-0-9955343-2-2

33. Bellows, H. A. (1936). The Poetic Edda: "Hovamol: The Ballad of the High One"

34. Thorpe, B. (trans.) (1866) Edda Sæmundar Hinns Froða: The Edda Of Sæmund The Learned. London: Trübner & Co.

35. see from http://www.odins-gift.com/pclass/havamalauden.htm

36. Sturluson, S., (1995) Edda, translated and edited

by Faulkes, A., London: Everyman, 1995, ISBN 0-460-87616-3

37. ante.

38. Forspjallsljóð (2002) translation and original retrieved from: https://notendur.hi.is/~eybjorn/ugm/hrg/hrg.html

FORTHCOMING
TITLES

THE BLOOD OF LÓÐURR AWAKENS
Power of the Midgard Man

The blood, DNA, flesh and physicality of our bodies are taken for granted by countless humans and envied by many others. We, the children of Yggdrasil (world tree) to whom Midgard (physical reality) was given at the time of our creation, hold deep and powerful secrets within ourselves and within our physical beings.

The Body (Lik), the Energy Body (Hamr) and the Shadow (Sal) form the great foundation of our own inner universe: our own creation. Understanding and mastering these physical parts of our Self provides us with such wonderful gifts that there are those in Creation who positively fear the prospect of our self-realisation.

The deep-seated secrets of centrality and balance are but a few of the wonders which await the reader. Mysteries of materialisation, realisation through inheritance and mysteries of our very blood will be revealed to all.

Learn all about their practical applications, their secrets and how to expand your Self through their proper use. Learn how to ground and materialise runic powers through them, how to manifest events in life by means of these three physical parts of your Self and learn why mankind is the envy of Creation.

255

HIGH GALDR: RUNE SCIENCE
The Sacred Science of the Gods

Runes, runes and more runes! The sacred science of the Gods, the runes were made available to their children, our Ancestors. Much information is available about the runes, yet so very little is known as to how they are actually used. They are chanted, they are written, and they are drawn. Yet all these methods fail to produce rapid or tangible manifestations.

Using the runes is a science and, like any science, the rules under which its principles operate need to be known. Unleashing a runic vocalisation using proper Galdr has been kept secret for ages, known to only an extremely select few who were capable of mastering their very Self. These methods for Galdr were passed down through generations as part of our vocal tradition, with only sparse written instruction preserved.

At long last, actual methods and underlying principles of manifesting the power of the runes are being made available unabridged with no hidden facets, no secret methods left unturned. Learn at long last how to wield the runes, how to unleash and manifest them, how to recode reality and reform events in life using the heritage left to us by our Ancestors and living within our DNA. Each and every rune holds a secret, a key, a power, a source of knowledge and a potential.

Learn to unleash it ALL with actual High Galdr.

www.ingramcontent.com/pod-product-compliance
Ingram Content Group UK Ltd.
Pitfield, Milton Keynes, MK11 3LW, UK
UKHW041402170225
4632UKWH00032B/143